Cambridge Elements ≡

Elements in Perception
edited by
James T. Enns
The University of British Columbia

CONSTRUCTING EXPERIENCE

Expectation and Attention in Perception

Jason Clarke
University of West London

CAMBRIDGE
UNIVERSITY PRESS

Shaftesbury Road, Cambridge CB2 8EA, United Kingdom

One Liberty Plaza, 20th Floor, New York, NY 10006, USA

477 Williamstown Road, Port Melbourne, VIC 3207, Australia

314–321, 3rd Floor, Plot 3, Splendor Forum, Jasola District Centre, New Delhi – 110025, India

103 Penang Road, #05–06/07, Visioncrest Commercial, Singapore 238467

Cambridge University Press is part of Cambridge University Press & Assessment, a department of the University of Cambridge.

We share the University's mission to contribute to society through the pursuit of education, learning and research at the highest international levels of excellence.

www.cambridge.org
Information on this title: www.cambridge.org/9781009588560

DOI: 10.1017/9781009588577

When citing this work, please include a reference to the DOI 10.1017/9781009588577

First published 2024

A catalogue record for this publication is available from the British Library

ISBN 978-1-009-58856-0 Hardback
ISBN 978-1-009-58855-3 Paperback
ISSN 2515-0502 (online)
ISSN 2515-0499 (print)

Constructing Experience

Expectation and Attention in Perception

Elements in Perception

DOI: 10.1017/9781009588577
First published online: December 2024

Jason Clarke
University of West London

Author for correspondence: Jason Clarke, Jason.Clarke@uwl.ac.uk

Abstract: This Element examines the influence of expectation and attention on conscious perception. It explores the debate on whether attention is necessary for conscious perception by presenting empirical evidence from studies on inattentional blindness, change blindness, and the attentional blink. While the evidence strongly suggests that attention is necessary for conscious perception, other research has shown that expectation can shape perception, sometimes leading to illusory experiences where predicted stimuli are perceived despite their absence. This phenomenon, termed 'expectation awareness', suggests that attention may not be necessary for all conscious experiences. These findings are explored within the predictive processing framework, where the brain is characterized as a prediction engine, continuously updating its internal models to minimize prediction errors. Integrating findings from psychology, neuroscience, and cognitive science, this Element provides a predictive processing model of how attention and expectation construct perceptual reality. It also discusses clinical and theoretical implications and suggests future research.

This Element also has a video abstract: www.cambridge.org/EPER-Clarke

Keywords: expectation, attention, consciousness, predictive processing, perception

ISBNs: 9781009588560 (HB), 9781009588553 (PB), 9781009588577 (OC)
ISSNs: 2515-0502 (online), 2515-0499 (print)

Contents

1 Introduction

What are you conscious of right *now*? Maybe you are sitting in a café near Piccadilly Circus, London reading this. You perceive a rich tapestry of sounds, sights, and smells: the aroma of coffee, the clinking of cups, and the vibrant decor. This detailed perception seems effortless, but studies suggest it may be an illusion, indicating we experience less than we think (Blackmore et al., 1995; Levin et al., 2000; Noe, 2002; O'Regan, 1992; Scholl et al., 2004; Ward, 2018).

The content of visual consciousness, whether rich or sparse in detail, and the necessary and sufficient cognitive and neural processes underlying any conscious experience remain hotly debated in the cognitive sciences (Block, 2011; Dehaene et al., 2006; Koch et al., 2016; Kouider et al., 2010; Lamme, 2018, 2010; Lenharo, 2023; Melloni et al., 2023; Pitts et al., 2018; Tononi & Koch, 2008). Resolving this debate is crucial for understanding conscious perception, with implications for psychology (Baars, 1997), neuroscience (Rees et al., 2002; Seth & Baynes, 2022), and artificial intelligence (AI) (Hassabis et al., 2017; LeCun et al., 2015). While it is widely accepted that attention influences conscious perception and can occur without consciousness (Cowey & Stoerig, 2004; Kentridge, 1999; Kentridge et al., 2004), and thus is not sufficient for conscious perception (see Noah & Mangun (2020) and Breitmeyer (2014) for reviews), the debate centres on whether attention is necessary for conscious perception.

Those on one side of the debate argue that without attention, there is no visual experience (Breitmeyer, 2014; Cohen & Dennett, 2011; Dehaene et al., 2006; Cohen et al., 2016; Mack & Rock, 1998). Evidence supporting this view comes from experimental research on inattentional blindness (IB), change blindness (CB), the attentional blink (AB), and event-related potentials (ERPs), electro-physiological markers of specific sensory, perceptual, cognitive, or motor events (Cohen et al., 2011; Dehaene et al., 2006; Lamme, 2003; Mack & Clarke, 2012; Mack & Rock, 1998; Rensink et al., 1997). These studies attest to the necessity of attention for visual experience.

On the other side of the debate is the view that visual consciousness is rich in informational content that does not require attention (Block, 1995; Koch & Tsuchiya, 2007; Lamme, 2004). Evidence for this perspective comes from paradigms where participants' conscious experiences are inferred from physiological markers, such as pupil size (Frassle et al., 2014; Kloosterman et al., 2015), without the need for explicit verbal reports (Koch et al., 2016; Tsuchiya et al., 2015), as well as ERP research. Additionally, findings from partial report paradigms and iconic memory (IM) experiments suggest that individuals can briefly access more visual information than they can attend to and report (Sperling,

1960). These have been put forward as supporting rich visual consciousness independent of attention (Block, 1995).

While this debate remains largely unresolved, growing experimental evidence reveals that visual consciousness is structured not only by attention but also by predictions or expectations about incoming sensory information. For example, expected stimuli are consciously perceived more quickly under conditions of continuous flash suppression than neutral or unexpected stimuli (Pinto et al., 2015). Attended objects in briefly presented scenes (100–200 ms) are often misperceived and interpreted as consistent with the scene gist, demonstrating the influence of expectations about scene schema on object perception (Mack et al., 2017).

Additionally and intriguingly, other studies reveal that observers often incorrectly report seeing an expected yet unattended stimulus in its absence (Aru et al., 2017; Aru et al., 2018; Erol et al., 2018; Mack et al., 2016). These findings suggest that while attention is necessary for conscious perception, it may not be required for non-veridical experiences, such as an imagined or hallucinated stimulus. The evidence suggests that expectations can generate illusory perceptions without attention (Aru et al., 2017; Aru et al., 2018; Erol et al., 2018; Mack et al., 2016).

One influential framework that can explain these findings is predictive processing (Friston, 2005; Hohwy, 2013; Hohwy & Seth, 2020). According to this framework, the brain is fundamentally a prediction machine that continuously generates and updates models of the world based on sensory inputs and prior experience (Friston, 2003; Friston, 2005). Perception, in this view, results from hierarchical precision-weighted prediction error minimization: a cascading top-down flow of predictions from abstract higher-level beliefs about the world to lower-level predictions at the level of sensory input, which infer the causal structure of the world from the noisy, ambiguous sensory input (Clark, 2015; Friston, 2010).

For example, suppose you wake up in an unfamiliar room, very dimly lit, and see a vague dark shape somewhere in the distance. Based on your experience with rooms, your brain predicts that the shape is indeed a chair. This high-level prediction is then compared to the sensory input. If there is a discrepancy between your prediction and the sensory input (say, if you move your head closer), a prediction error arises. If the prediction error is deemed reliable, it prompts the brain to adjust its predictions, refining your perception of the shape. This process continues hierarchically, from high-level predictions about the object being a chair to lower-level sensory details, such as the chair's contours and texture, until the prediction error is minimized and a coherent perception occurs. You perceive a chair.

In this context, a generative model is the brain's internal framework that predicts sensory inputs. Prediction errors, the differences between predicted and actual inputs, are weighted by their precision or estimated reliability. Minimizing these prediction errors involves integrating bottom-up sensory signals with top-down expectations (Friston, 2005).

According to this theory, our experiences are shaped by the parameters of the generative model, which are the variables, states, and structures within the brain that determine how predictions are generated and updated. These parameters include synaptic weights, connectivity patterns between neurons, and the encoding of prior expectations. All of these factors influence how the brain processes sensory inputs and minimizes prediction errors. This system is continually adjusted based on precision-weighted prediction errors, driving learning and perception. This approach offers a promising way to integrate perception, imagination, attention, cognition, and consciousness into a comprehensive framework (Clark, 2013; Jones & Wilkinson, 2020).

In this Element, we explore the cognitive processes and neural mechanisms that underpin the construction of perceptual experience. We will examine the relationship between attention and conscious experience, the role of expectation in shaping perception, and the combined effects of both. To clarify terminology at the outset: *Attention* will initially be discussed in line with the broader literature – considering it as limited in capacity, selective, and directed endogenously or exogenously. However, we will ultimately define attention as variable precision weightings of prediction errors. *Expectation* will be defined as learned or perhaps hardwired predictions that the brain generates based on prior knowledge, contextual cues, and past experiences. By *experience*, we mean *awareness* or *consciousness* in perception, dreams, hallucinations, and imagination, and we use these terms synonymously. Here, we focus specifically on visual experience. Visual experience can range from being aware of object properties (colour, texture, orientation, motion, and depth) to objects (faces, dogs, chairs, and cars) and scenes (busy intersections in a city, classrooms, farms, and forests).

Following an introduction to consciousness and perception and relevant issues in these fields (Sections 2 and 3), we will discuss in some detail experiments from our lab and those of others exploring the role of attention in visual scene and object perception (Section 4). We will argue that the weight of evidence suggests that attention is necessary for conscious perception. In the next section (Section 5), we will explore how expectations influence what we perceive and how they can lead us to see what we expect rather than what is given in the stimulus. Following this, we will explore how these two processes interact to influence conscious perception (Section 6).

Finally (Section 7), and this may be what is of central interest in this Element, in some experiments demonstrating the necessity of attention for conscious perception, an intriguing and unexpected result emerged: when participants were attending to a visually demanding task and queried about what they had seen in an unattended location, they often reported seeing stimuli (a grid of letters, a coloured circle, and a face) that were not, in fact, present. This was driven by their expectations from prior repeated trials in which the stimuli had been presented. We termed this phenomenon of an illusory perception without attention 'Expectation Awareness'. These findings suggest that while attention is necessary for perception, it may not be required for all forms of conscious experience. Using a simple computational model, we will show how these findings can be explained within the predictive coding framework, where the allocation of precision to prediction errors (attention) and predictions (expectation) determines the contents of experience. In the concluding section (Section 8), we will briefly discuss the implications for current scientific theories of consciousness as well as clinical applications.

2 Consciousness

2.1 Introduction

From the moment we wake until we fall into a dreamless sleep, our brain constructs experiences ranging from the vibrant hues of a sunrise to the surreal narratives of dreams. Defining and measuring consciousness is fraught with difficulties. Indeed, consciousness has been described as a slippery term (Blackmore, 2005), referring to various phenomena such as self-awareness, reflective thought, and sensory perception. Another difficulty is that, unlike other phenomena in the sciences, consciousness is not publicly observable, making it challenging to study objectively. A frequently cited definition in the literature which seems to intuitively capture what consciousness is comes from Thomas Nagel's seminal paper 'What is it like to be a bat?' (Nagel, 1974). According to Nagel, a system is conscious if there is something it is like to *be* that system – for example, if it experiences temperature, colours, sounds, or smells. Presumably, there is nothing it is like to be a thermostat or a mobile phone; however, there is something it is like to be a human or another animal, such as a bat. In the case of humans, there is subjective experience: the blinding white of fresh snow, the tanginess of a lemon, the warmth of sunshine on skin, and the pain of a bee sting. In this Element, when we discuss consciousness, experience, or awareness, we are referring specifically to visual experience: awareness of colours, objects, motion, faces, and scenes.

2.2 Phenomenal and Access Consciousness

A distinction is often made between phenomenal and access consciousness (Block, 1995; Block, 2007). Phenomenal consciousness refers to subjective qualities, such as the vivid redness of a sunset or the itchiness of a wool sweater. In contrast, access consciousness refers to the computational, functional, neurological, and behavioural mechanisms that underlie how we report, make decisions, remember, and use information about experiences. For example, recognizing and reporting that we are seeing a red sunset and deciding to alleviate an itch involves access consciousness.

Whether this distinction can be made remains a prominent issue in consciousness research (Kouider et al., 2010). The argument centres on whether we are conscious of more information than we have cognitive access to. One perspective is that phenomenal consciousness 'overflows' access consciousness (Block, 2011). In other words, observers have a richer phenomenology – the subjective experience of sensory qualities – than can be accessed by cognitive processes such as attention, working memory, and reporting mechanisms (Amir et al., 2023; Block, 1995; Block, 2005; Lamme, 2004).

Conversely, others argue against the overflow hypothesis, challenging the distinction between phenomenal and access consciousness (Cohen & Dennett, 2011; Dehaene et al., 2006; Kouider et al., 2010; Naccache, 2018; Overgaard, 2018). According to these researchers, the functions of consciousness (access consciousness) exhaust its nature. There is no consciousness without function. Under such accounts, an overflow of phenomenal consciousness is an illusion (Kouider et al., 2017).

2.3 Levels and Contents of Consciousness

Another important and contested distinction is between global states (also called levels) and local states or the contents of consciousness (Bayne et al., 2016; Hohwy, 2009; Koch et al., 2016). Global states refer to varying states of awareness, ranging from full alertness to unconsciousness. These include wakefulness, sleep, dreaming, anaesthesia, coma, vegetative state, and locked-in syndrome, each characterized by distinct neural activity and behavioural patterns (Laureys, 2005; Laureys et al., 2015). The contents of consciousness encompass the objects, sounds, smells, and scenes represented in experience at any given moment. These include sensory perceptions (seeing a cat, hearing it meow), emotions (feeling happy to see the cat), thoughts (thinking about preparing food for the cat), memories (recalling seeing the cat for the first time), hallucinations (seeing the cat when it is not there), and the contents of imagination (seeing the cat flying with wings).

Research suggests that global states and contents of consciousness are inter-related (Aru et al., 2019). Conscious content depends on the global state. For example, degraded levels of consciousness, such as those experienced in min-imally conscious states (MCS), often reduce the vividness and clarity of con-scious contents (Overgaard & Overgaard, 2010). Different global states might gate or limit the range of conscious contents, affecting the quality and extent of what is experienced. This gating mechanism can result in varying degrees of richness in conscious experience across different states, revealing an inter-dependence between local (content) and global states (Bayne et al., 2016).

2.4 Measuring the Contents of Consciousness

In the laboratory, experimentalists treat consciousness as a variable and create situations where participants are either aware or unaware of a stimulus. Known as the contrastive method, this approach allows researchers to compare con-scious and unconscious processing. By creating conditions where participants are aware of the stimulus and others where they are not, researchers can isolate the neural and cognitive mechanisms underlying conscious perception from those underlying unconscious processing (Baars, 1993). Here, some of the standard ways of achieving this are briefly described (for a more exhaustive review, see Kim & Blake (2005), Bachmann et al. (2011), and Bachmann & Aru (2023)). We will refer to some of these techniques throughout this Element.

Masking: A mask is another visual stimulus that is presented either before or after the target stimulus to interfere with its processing. By manipulating the interval between the target and the mask, researchers can effectively 'mask' the target, studying the conditions under which it is consciously and not consciously perceived (Breitmeyer, 2007; Breitmeyer & Ogmen, 2006). This allows for the differentiation between neural activity associated with unconscious and con-scious processing. Different kinds of masking techniques are used to achieve this effect. Backward masking involves presenting the mask following the target stimulus, which interferes with the processing of the target and prevents it from reaching conscious awareness. Forward masking involves presenting the mask before the target stimulus, affecting the processing of the subsequent target. In metacontrast masking, the mask does not spatially overlap the target but closely follows it in time, while surrounding it spatially, reducing target visibility. Finally, sandwich masking involves presenting the target stimulus between two masks, one before and one after. These variations of masking help researchers dissect the temporal dynamics of visual processing and the condi-tions under which stimuli are consciously and unconsciously perceived (Breitmeyer, 2007; Breitmeyer, 2014). As well as measuring the threshold for conscious perception, many masking studies employ accuracy or sensitivity as the dependent measure.

Binocular Rivalry: In this method, each eye is shown a different image: a house to the left eye and a face to the right eye, for instance. Instead of perceiving an amalgamation of house and face, perception vacillates: sometimes, the participant reports seeing a face and sometimes a house. Using this method, experimentalists can measure the processes underlying conscious perception by comparing the activity when the participants are conscious of the stimulus to when they are not while keeping the sensory input constant. This contrast allows researchers to differentiate the neural activity associated with conscious perception (when one image is dominant) from that associated with unconscious processing (when the image is suppressed). For example, studies show that neural activity in the visual, parietal, and prefrontal cortex correlates with alternating perceptions during binocular rivalry (Blake & Logothetis, 2002). Through such research, researchers can identify the neural correlates of visual conscious perception (Logothetis et al., 1996; Sterzer et al., 2009; Tong et al., 2006).

Inattentional Blindness: Inattentional blindness (IB) occurs when an observer is unaware of a visible stimulus because their attention is engaged elsewhere (Mack & Rock, 1998; Most et al., 2001; Most et al., 2005). Paradigms of IB reveal the limits of attention and conscious perception and illustrate how unattended stimuli can evade awareness. A classic example is a study by Simons and Chabris (1999), where participants watched a video of people passing a basketball and failed to notice a person in a gorilla suit walking through the scene, a striking example of the limitation of conscious perception. Inattentional blindness provides researchers with a tool for investigating the selective nature of attention and the mechanisms by which certain stimuli fail to enter consciousness (Jensen et al., 2011).

Visual Illusions: Visual illusions are an important tool in studying consciousness as they reveal the rules and logic of the construction of percepts. They occur when there is a discrepancy between the external reality and our experience of it and thus give insight into how the brain interprets sensory information to create a perception. Motion-induced blindness presents one such tool. In this illusion, a salient constantly present stimulus in the visual field perceptually disappears and appears when surrounded by a moving pattern. By contrasting neural activity when the static stimulus is visible (conscious processing) and when it disappears (unconscious processing), researchers can reveal the cognitive and neural processes associated with conscious perception (e.g., Bonneh, Cooperman, and Sagi (2001)).

Continuous Flash Suppression (CFS): By rapidly presenting a series of images to one eye while showing a static image to the other, researchers can suppress the perception of the static image for several seconds. For example, in one CFS study, Jiang, Costello, and He (2007) demonstrated that emotional faces break through suppression faster than neutral faces, indicating that certain stimuli have privileged access to consciousness due to their emotional salience. Other CFS research reveals that high-level visual processes can occur without conscious perception. For example, in an fMRI study, Sterzer et al. (2008) found that the category of objects invisible to participants due to CFS was still encoded in high-level visual areas, such as the fusiform face area (FFA) and the parahippocampal place area (PPA), indicating that such processing can occur without conscious perception.

Attentional Blink (AB): Attentional blink is a phenomenon where an observer fails to detect a second stimulus presented within 200–500 milliseconds after the first stimulus. This occurs because processing the first stimulus occupies attentional resources, creating a temporary 'blink' during which the second stimulus is missed (Raymond, Shapiro, & Arnell, 1992). By comparing neural activity during the blink period (unconscious processing) to when the second stimulus is detected (conscious processing), researchers can study the temporal dynamics of attention and its role in conscious perception. Researchers have found that the AB can reveal how attentional resources are allocated over time and how this affects awareness (Martens & Wyble, 2010).

Using these paradigms and many others, experimenters can measure thresholds for the conscious perception of different stimuli, determine when stimuli enter awareness, and explore the conditions under which stimuli are consciously perceived. Additionally, isolating the psychological and neural processes that occur when stimuli are consciously perceived versus when they are not allows researchers to uncover the neural correlates of consciousness (NCC), the minimal neuronal mechanisms jointly sufficient for a specific conscious experience (Dehaene & Changeux, 2011; Koch et al., 2016).

In the next section, we will explore the cognitive and neural underpinnings of perception and how the brain's predictive and inferential mechanisms create perceptual reality. With this foundational understanding, we will go on to examine the roles of attention, expectation, and their interplay in conscious perception, building on the concepts introduced here and integrating them within a theoretical framework, which is introduced in the following section.

3 Perception

3.1 Introduction

Gazing upwards as we lie in a park on a sunny day, we perceive the colours, textures, and motion of the leaves against a blue sky. We do not see a flat scene (the two-dimensional image on the retina) but one with spatial and temporal depth: the leaves nearby may be perceived as within arm's reach, while those higher in the tree are perceived as relatively further away. Encased in the skull, the brain's point of contact with the world beyond is the relentless barrage of information from that world impinging on sensory receptors. In the case of vision, light is reflected from the three-dimensional world (the distal stimulus) and forms a two-dimensional image on the retina (the proximal stimulus). From this sensory input pattern, the brain faces the challenge of recovering the distal stimulus (the cause of the input) from the proximal stimulus (its effect on the sensory receptors) (Hohwy, 2013; Marr, 1982). This involves moving from two dimensions to three, which is not a well-defined function since each point in the 2D image could correspond to an infinite number of points in the 3D environment. An infinite number of three-dimensional objects of different sizes, shapes, slopes, and slants at various distances could create an identical two-dimensional image on the retina (Figure 1). Given this, how does the brain recover the world out there from the highly ambiguous input? How does it determine the cause from its effect on the retina when that effect has multiple possible causes?

This can be illustrated with bistable figures, two-dimensional stimuli alternately perceived as two different three-dimensional objects (Blake & Logothetis, 2002), such as the Necker Cube (see Figure 2). Given on the retina is a two-dimensional shape, yet we perceive a three-dimensional cube. Moreover, continued observation changes our perception of the cube, revealing a new orientation. The perception of bistable figures demonstrates that the brain cannot settle on a single interpretation of the retinal image, revealing the inherent ambiguity in the visual input and the constructive nature of perception. When viewing bistable figures, we experience this in real time.

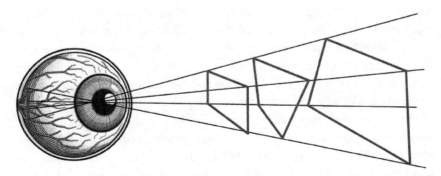

Figure 1 The inverse problem: reconstructing three-dimensional space from two-dimensional retinal images.

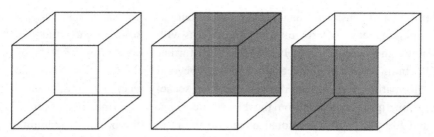

Figure 2 Necker Cube (left) demonstrating perceptual bistability. The centre and right cubes illustrate different perceptual interpretations, where the shaded surfaces represent possible front and rear faces of the cube, leading to alternative 3D perceptions depending on which face is seen as being in front.

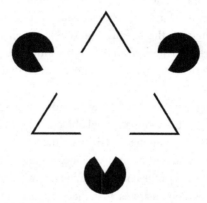

Figure 3 Kanizsa triangle illustrating illusory contours.

Furthermore, visual illusions illustrate how what we perceive is not strictly determined by the pattern of stimulation in the retinal input. In the Kanizsa triangle, we perceive an illusory white triangle superimposed on three circles (see Figure 3). We can see the edges of the triangle, which appears to be whiter than its white background. However, if we take a photometer and measure the luminance profile of the 'triangle', we will see there is no change in luminance between what we perceive as the edges and the background. The triangle is a construction of your visual system.

This inverse problem of vision, recovering the causal structure of the three-dimensional external world from the two-dimensional sensory input, has been recognized historically (Berkeley, 1948), as has the constructive nature of experience (Kant, 2001/1783; Swanson, 2016). Helmholtz introduced unconscious inference, a process of unconscious calculations to interpret highly ambiguous sensory input (Helmholtz, 1867/1925). He proposed the likelihood principle: perceptual systems favour the interpretation of sensory data most consistent with expectations. For example, suppose you see a vague shape moving in a forest. In that case, your brain is more likely to interpret it as an animal rather than an inanimate object because, based on past experiences, it is more probable that moving shapes in such contexts are living creatures. This probabilistic approach allows the brain to construct a coherent representation of the world, even when the sensory input is ambiguous or incomplete. As discussed later, Helmholtz's unconscious inference and likelihood principle remain foundational in contemporary theories of perception (Clark, 2013).

3.2 Bottom-up and Top-down Processing

Perception involves the interaction of bottom-up and top-down processes. Bottom-up processing refers to the sensory-driven aspects of perception, where information from the sensory receptors is relayed to the brain for further processing. This begins with sensory input, building a percept through a series of hierarchical stages – that is, from cells that encode light and dark in the retina to cells in early cortical areas that encode lines and edges, to cells in higher visual areas that encode faces and objects (Marr, 1982). Perception is thus seen as a process of integrating sensory inputs through multiple levels of processing in a feed-forward direction: basic features such as colour, brightness, edges, and motion providing the building blocks for high-level representations such as faces, objects, and scenes.

In contrast, top-down processing involves cognitive factors such as expectations and knowledge based on prior experiences. Top-down processes can modify or shape sensory information, leading to perceptual interpretations that align with expectations and prior knowledge. This type of processing is conceptually driven and helps resolve ambiguities in sensory input by applying learned information and contextual clues (Bar, 2004; Gregory, 1980; Kersten et al., 2004).

A demonstration of the interrelation between bottom-up and top-down processing can be seen in Figure 4. Upon first seeing such a stimulus, observers do not see much, just the blotches of black and white that make up the stimulus However, if we keep looking, we perceive this array of black and white blotches as a Dalmatian dog, perhaps in dappled sunlight, sniffing its way along a path. Here, we see top-down processes – predictions about the world based on past experience – interacting with the bottom-up input, the ambiguous image on the retina, shaping what we perceive. Now, whenever you look at the image, you will most likely perceive it as the dog. Note that the image does not have a dog

Perception

Figure 4 Perceptual illusion demonstrating a hidden Dalmatian dog.

shape. Our brains infer it is there, and this inference determines what we perceive. This shows the powerful influence of top-down processing in interpreting and making sense of ambiguous sensory information. Prior knowledge and expectations can significantly shape our perceptual experience.

3.3 Bottom-Up Theories of Perception

How much influence do bottom-up processes and top-down processes have on what we perceive? Bottom-up theories of perception emphasize the role of sensory input in shaping perceptual experience. Traditionally, this process has been considered to work roughly in the following way: sensory information impinges on the retina, which is the first step in a chain of (mostly) feed-forward information processing from the retina via the optic nerve to the back of the brain, the occipital cortex, and on to the temporal lobes. Perception is seen as a bottom-up process: from processing simple light/dark distinctions at the retinal level, to cells that are sensitive to edges and line orientation, colour, motion, and spatial frequencies, and at higher levels (i.e., those in the temporal lobe), cells that respond to faces, objects, and scenes. In seminal studies for which they won the Nobel Prize, Hubel and Wiesel demonstrated that cells in the retina of anaesthetized cats responded to spots of light located in very specific areas of the retina, while cells in the visual cortex responded to edges, or lines composed of these spots of light again located in very specific areas of the retina (e.g., Hubel & Wiesel, 1959). Later work revealed that as one moved further away from the retinal input in the visual system, cells responded to visual features, and became increasingly specialized in responding to faces, tools, scenes, and objects (e.g., Hubel & Wiesel, 1962; Kanwisher et al., 1997; Grill-Spector & Malach, 2004). Such a flow of information, in which simple light–dark distinctions lead to edge detection and object perception and recognition, from the visually simple to the more complex, suggests that perceptions are constructed from the sensory input in an ascending hierarchy of layers of information processing.

An influential bottom-up theory is David Marr's computational approach to vision (Marr, 1982), which describes vision as a series of information-processing stages that transform raw visual input into a detailed, three-dimensional representation. Marr's model includes several key stages:

- The Primal Sketch: This stage captures basic features such as edges, textures, and simple geometric structures, representing these features in a way that highlights the intensity changes in the visual field.
- The 2.5D Sketch: This stage integrates information about depth and surface orientation, adding a sense of the spatial layout by incorporating depth cues like shading, texture gradients, and binocular disparity, providing a viewer-centred representation of the scene.
- The 3D Model Representation: This final stage integrates the information from the 2.5D sketch to form a complete, three-dimensional understanding of the visual scene, allowing for recognition and manipulation of objects regardless of the viewer's perspective.

For example, consider a coffee cup on a table: at the primal sketch stage, the visual system detects the edges of the coffee cup, the handle, and the table, identifying the boundaries where there is a significant change in light intensity, outlining the shapes present in the scene. At the 2.5D sketch stage, depth cues are added to the visual representation, incorporating information about the curvature of the cup, the roundness of the handle, and the angle of the table surface. Finally, at the 3D model representation stage, the brain constructs a detailed three-dimensional model of the scene, recognizing the coffee cup as a distinct object, understanding its three-dimensional form, and allowing the viewer to recognize the cup, anticipate how it can be picked up, and understand its spatial relationship with other objects on the table. By processing visual information through these stages, Marr's computational approach demonstrates how the brain transforms raw sensory input into a rich, three-dimensional representation.

This model underscores a predominantly bottom-up process in visual perception, where the interpretation of our visual world is assembled in a hierarchical fashion, layer by layer, culminating in the rich tapestry of the reality we perceive. But does this account for the flipping of perception when viewing the Necker Cube? Does this account for the ghostly edges one sees when looking at the Kanizsa triangle? Can this bottom-up explanation account for all experiences?

3.4 Top-Down Theories of Perception

According to perhaps the most widely accepted theory of vision, perception is a construction created mainly by top-down hypothesis-generating mechanisms, whose predictions are based on expectations (Clark, 2013; Gregory, 1980; Hohwy, 2013; Hohwy, 2020; Seth, 2021). Expectations are foundational components of internal models which predict the cause of sensory input (Series & Seitz, 2013; Summerfield & Egner, 2009). According to such accounts, the nervous system is essentially a prediction machine that attempts to minimize surprise (errors between the predictions and the sensory information, i.e., expectation violations) and maximize expectation (Friston et al., 2012) using a form of Bayesian inference (Knill & Pouget, 2004).

3.5 Bayesian Inference and Predictive Coding

Today, modern computational theories are beginning to provide a detailed account of how perception is constructed from prior knowledge and sensory input. While predictive processing encompasses the broad principle that the brain is continuously generating and updating predictions about sensory inputs, predictive coding (Mumford, 1992; Rao & Ballard,1999) specifically involves a process of precision-weighted prediction error minimization through hierarchical Bayesian inference (Clark, 2013; Friston, 2005; Hohwy, 2013). According to this framework, what we perceive results from this precision-weighted prediction error minimization process.

Bayes' theorem is fundamental to this framework. Originating from the work of Thomas Bayes in the eighteenth century, it provides a mathematical foundation for updating beliefs about a hypothesis based on new evidence (Bayes, 1763; Jeffreys, 1998). Bayes' theorem formalizes this process:

$$P(H \mid E) = P(E \mid H) \times P(H) / P(E),$$

where

P(H|E) is the posterior probability, the updated probability of the hypothesis *H* given the evidence *E*.

P(E|H) is the likelihood, the probability of observing the evidence *E* if the hypothesis *H* is true.

$P(H)$ is the prior probability, the initial probability of the hypothesis before seeing the evidence.

$P(E)$ is the marginal likelihood, the total probability of the evidence under all possible hypotheses.

To illustrate, consider this – you hear a scratching noise. What is it? This sound could originate from multiple sources (the inverse problem). Is it rain tapping on the window, a cat scratching at the door, or a tree branch scraping against the outside wall? Using Bayes' theorem, your brain evaluates the likelihood of each source based on prior knowledge and current sensory input. If you live in a quiet area with no history of break-ins, the probability $P(H)$ of a burglar being the source is low. Conversely, if you know trees often scrape against your wall when windy, this prior probability is higher. Combining these priors with the evidence likelihood $P(E|H)$, your brain updates its belief to identify the most probable noise source.

In predictive coding, approximate Bayesian inference is used due to the computational challenges of exact Bayesian inference (Friston, 2010). According to this theory, the brain generates predictions about expected input at each hierarchical level, comparing these predictions to the input at the level below to calculate prediction errors (mismatches between the prediction and the sensory input). These errors are propagated up the hierarchy to refine future predictions (Clark, 2013). This process minimizes prediction errors, enhancing perception and action efficiency. Lower levels process basic sensory features, while higher levels integrate these into detailed representations, generating predictions for the level below (Clark, 2015; Friston, 2005; Millidge et al., 2022) (see Figure 5). The result is an informationally rich model of the world inside the brain.

Generative models, central to predictive coding, simulate expected sensory signals, encapsulating statistical regularities of sensory inputs. When sensory input mismatches predictions, prediction errors signal the need to update generative models. These errors are propagated up the hierarchy, adjusting higher-level predictions to better predict lower-level activity (Rao & Ballard, 1999).

Precision weighting adjusts the influence of prediction errors based on reliability. In statistical terms, precision is the inverse of variance, representing the confidence in the accuracy of sensory inputs. High-precision errors (reliable inputs) weigh more in updating models, while low-precision errors (noisy inputs) are downplayed. This allows for prioritization of important information (Yon & Frith, 2021). For example, in dim light, the brain relies more on prior

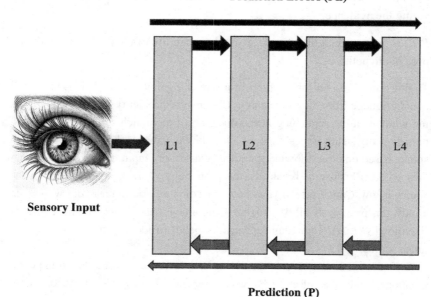

Prediction Errors (PE)

Sensory Input

Prediction (P)

Figure 5 Hierarchical processing of sensory input through prediction and
prediction error across multiple layers.

knowledge than unclear sensory evidence, demonstrating the adaptive nature of
perception under varying conditions.

Predictive coding frames perception as an active process of hypothesis
testing and error correction. Navigating your way through the busy city
streets, your brain uses internal models from past experiences to predict the
movement of people around you. Sensory input about their movements is
continuously compared to these predictions, and discrepancies (prediction
errors) are used to update the model. This hierarchical process involves
basic motion predictions and interpretations of complex social behaviour,
with precision weighting prioritizing reliable information (Friston, 2010).
Similarly, in a fast-paced environment like driving, your brain predicts the
behaviour of other vehicles based on their speed and trajectory. As the
situation evolves, these predictions are updated using incoming visual data.
Precision weighting helps the brain prioritize the most reliable information,
such as the immediate visual feedback of other cars' positions, enabling swift
and accurate reactions (Yon & Frith, 2021).

Helmholtz's theory of unconscious inference laid the foundation for understanding perception as an active inferential process. He proposed that the brain

interprets sensory input by inferring the most likely causes based on prior knowledge and sensory data. Predictive coding builds on this idea, suggesting that the brain continuously generates and updates predictions about the environment, minimizing prediction errors through Bayesian inference. Thus, predictive coding can be seen as a modern extension of Helmholtz's theories, integrating them with contemporary computational and neuroscientific approaches to explain how the brain constructs perceptual reality.

In the following section, we will explore how attention shapes conscious perception. We will then investigate the role of expectation in visual experience and the interaction between attention and expectation.

4 Attention

4.1 Attention and Perception

Attention has limited capacity, allowing us to attend to about three to four objects simultaneously (Cowan, 2001; Luck & Vogel, 1997). While detailed processing of individual objects is limited, larger ensembles or global patterns can be processed more extensively as summary statistics (Jackson-Nielsen et al., 2017). This trade-off shows that the number of objects attended to and the detail processed are inversely related. Perceptual load, the quantity and complexity of information we can attend to simultaneously, affects our ability to process unattended information (Lavie, 2005). Attention can be directed at spatial locations (Posner, 1980), objects (Egly, Driver, & Rafal, 1994), or features like colour or shape (Saenz, Buracas, & Boynton, 2002). Attention enhances spatial and temporal resolution, contrast sensitivity, and feature binding, and reduces crowding (Carrasco & McElree, 2001; Carrasco et al., 2002; He, Cavanagh, & Intriligator, 1996; Treisman & Gelade, 1980; Yeshurun & Carrasco, 1998). It also modulates sensory processing, enhancing neural activity related to attended stimuli while suppressing that of unattended stimuli (Desimone & Duncan, 1995).

Attention can be overt (directly focusing sensory organs) or covert (mentally focusing without physical movement) (Posner, 1980). Covert attention, such as spatially focused covert attention, involves focusing on a location without eye movements (Posner, 1980).

Attention is also categorized as endogenous (internally driven) or exogenous (externally driven) (Corbetta & Shulman, 2002). Selective attention focuses on locations, objects, features, or tasks while ignoring others, as seen in listening to one conversation at a noisy party (Broadbent, 1958), and can also be distributed across multiple elements simultaneously, like tracking players in a sports game (Neisser & Becklen, 1975).

4.2 Neural Mechanisms of Attention

A theory of attention proposed by Desimone and Duncan (1995) has been highly influential in the cognitive sciences. According to this model, the flood of incoming visual data competes for limited neural representation. Attention enhances the processing of a stimulus by biasing the competition in favour of the attended stimulus. For example, studies show that attention increases visual responses in the extrastriate visual cortex (e.g., V4) by boosting the activity of neurons representing the attended stimulus while suppressing the activity of neurons representing competing stimuli (Luck et al., 1997; Reynolds et al., 2000). This modulation has also been observed in other regions, including the prefrontal cortex and the lateral intraparietal area (Bisley & Goldberg, 2010; Buschman & Miller, 2007). The biased competition model integrates both top-down and bottom-up processing in selective attention. Top-down processes involve cognitive control from higher brain regions that bias the competition based on the individual's goals and expectations. Bottom-up processes are driven by the properties of the stimulus, such as its salience and novelty.

In predictive coding, attention has been conceptualized as precision, the accuracy or reliability (more precisely, the inverse variance) of specific sensory signals in the context of prediction errors (Hohwy, 2012; but see Aitchison & Lengyel (2017) for a differing perspective). According to this perspective, attention enhances the reliability of prediction errors by assigning greater weight to specific sensory inputs over others. By increasing the precision of relevant information, attention helps the brain minimize prediction errors more effectively, leading to a more accurate perception of the world (Feldman & Friston, 2010). For example, Kok et al. (2012) conducted a study where they manipulated attention and prediction independently using an fMRI setup and found that attention boosts the precision of perceptual inference, enhancing the neural response to predicted stimuli when they are attended compared to when they are unattended. This interaction supports the view that attention increases the synaptic gain of neurons representing sensory data (prediction errors), thus optimizing perceptual accuracy (Feldman & Friston, 2010; Kok et al., 2011). We will explore this in more detail in later sections.

4.3 The Debate over the Necessity of Attention for Conscious Perception

As the Introduction outlines, a debate persists in the cognitive sciences regarding the relationship between attention and conscious perception (Block, 2011; Lamme, 2010; Koch & Tsuchiya, 2007). In this section, we will examine evidence from various experimental paradigms to explore whether attention is necessary for conscious perception. We begin by discussing findings from studies on inattentional blindness (IB), change blindness (CB), the attentional blink (AB), and ERP research suggesting that attention is necessary for conscious perception. Next, we present counterarguments based on research indicating that consciousness can occur without attention, focusing on summary statistics, gist perception, ERPs, and iconic memory (IM). Finally, we critically evaluate evidence from both sides and argue that the weight of evidence suggests that attention is necessary for conscious perception.

4.3.1 Consciousness Requires Attention

Inattentional Blindness

Compelling evidence for the necessity of attention for conscious perception comes from research on IB (Mack & Rock, 1998; Simons & Chabris, 1999). In Mack and Rock's seminal experiments, participants were briefly presented with a horizontal/vertical cross on a computer screen, either at fixation (the centre of the screen) or several degrees of visual angle away. Their task was to report which arm of the cross (horizontal or vertical) was more extended. This demanding task involved a slight difference between arm lengths, and the brief stimulus presentation (200 ms) precluded visual exploration by saccadic eye movements. On the critical trial, an unexpected stimulus was presented with the cross. participants were questioned about anything else they had seen after reporting the more extended arm.

When the stimulus (e.g., a small square) was presented parafoveally in the visual periphery, around 25 per cent of participants failed to see it. Surprisingly, when the stimulus was at fixation, around 75 per cent of participants failed to see it. This greater IB to stimuli at fixation was explained by active inhibition. Typically, attention and eye movements are aligned (attention is deployed where the eyes are fixating, as when the stimulus is at the centre of the screen). However, when the cross appears in the visual periphery, attention to where the eyes are fixated must be inhibited to be deployed to the peripheral location (see Mack & Rock (1998, chapter 4) for evidence of active inhibition).

Studies using IB paradigms show that conscious perception of visual features, such as motion, flicker, colour, size, and integration of stimulus contours depends on attention (Mack & Rock, 1998; Pitts et al., 2012), as well as face perception (Shafto & Pitts, 2015). In their landmark study, Most et al. (2001) examined the role of similarity in IB. They demonstrated that the more similar an unexpected object is to attended items, and the greater its difference from ignored items, the more likely it is to be noticed, revealing the importance of both selective attention and selective ignoring in the detection of unexpected stimuli. Their results showed that when the unexpected object had the same luminance as the attended items, it was more likely to be detected, whereas similarity to ignored items reduced detection rates significantly.

Building on these findings, Most et al. (2005) further explored how attentional sets influence IB. They discovered that unexpected objects are more likely to be noticed when they share features with the attended set. For example, in a dynamic visual task, participants were more likely to notice an unexpected object when it matched the colour of the attended items. This research emphasized that attentional sets can be highly specific and that detection of unexpected objects depends on the alignment of these sets with the features of the objects.

Ding et al. (2024) provided additional insights by examining all three aspects of similarity: similarity to attended items, similarity to ignored items, and similarity between attended and ignored items. Their experiments demonstrated that similarity to both attended and ignored items affects noticing, with a greater impact from similarity to ignored items. They found that the degree of similarity to ignored shapes significantly influences noticing rates, suggesting that suppression mechanisms play a critical role in IB. This study reveals evidence of an interplay between enhancement of attended items and suppression of ignored items in visual processing (see also Wood & Simons (2017)).

Further supporting the necessity of attention for conscious perception, Mack and Clarke (2012) conducted four experiments to explore whether gist perception, defined as the ability to rapidly extract and recognize a scene, occurs without attention. Participants were shown grayscale images of natural scenes, flashed on a computer screen for brief durations of 100 ms centrally or 200 ms peripherally, followed by a mask. In the inattention condition, participants reported the longer arm of a cross flashed briefly in one of the four quadrants of the screen. This cross was accompanied by a grayscale mosaic pattern at the centre of the screen. After several non-critical trials, the critical trial followed, where participants performed the same task, and a scene replaced the grayscale pattern. After reporting the longer arm of the cross, participants were asked if they had seen anything else. In the divided attention condition, participants reported both the longer arm of the cross and anything else seen on the screen. In the full attention condition, participants ignored the cross and reported anything else presented. Across all experiments, only 17 per cent of participants reported seeing the gist of the scene in the inattention condition, compared to 65 per cent in the divided attention condition and 82 per cent in the full attention condition. Importantly, in the inattention condition, most participants not only failed to report gist, but also were not aware of anything different from prior trials.

These results were corroborated by earlier findings from Cohen et al. (2011). They investigated whether natural scene perception requires attention using multiple object tracking (MOT) and rapid serial visual presentation (RSVP) tasks. In the first experiment, participants tracked four of eight black discs moving at 10.5° per second while background images changed every 67 ms, demanding continuous attention. On the critical fifth trial, a natural scene replaced the mask, and 64 per cent of participants experienced IB, while only 18 per cent detected it. In subsequent trials, when explicitly asked to detect and classify scenes, they correctly identified scenes 96 per cent of the time, indicating that IB was due to attentional allocation. In the second part of the experiment, participants counted digits in a rapidly presented stream of letters (RSVP task), with backgrounds alternating every 100 ms. On the critical fifth trial, 50 per cent of participants experienced IB, with only 23 per cent detecting the scene immediately. During post-IB trials, participants identified scenes 93 per cent of the time. The second experiment combined the MOT task with scene classification, showing that at 4.5° per second, scene perception was unimpaired, suggesting minimal attention is needed. However, at 10.5° per second, performance on the scene task decreased, indicating significant attentional requirements. In the third experiment, participants counted digits in the RSVP stream while performing scene detection and categorization tasks, with each stream containing twelve to seventeen displays, each lasting 100 ms. Results showed significant performance drops under dual-task conditions: an 11 per cent drop in the five-category classification task and a 26 per cent drop in the animal-vehicle discrimination task, indicating that different aspects of scene perception require varying levels of attention.

Taken together, the studies by Mack and Clarke (2012) and Cohen et al. (2011) provide strong evidence that conscious perception of scenes requires attention. Their findings demonstrated significant rates of IB and dual-task interference when participants' attention was fully engaged by demanding tasks. These results challenge the idea that natural scenes can be perceived preattentively and demonstrate the critical role of attention in visual awareness.

Webster et al. (2018) demonstrated that canonical coloured, luminance, and orientation significantly reduce IB to scenes, indicating that expected visual features facilitate conscious perception of scenes. Their research shows that when attentional demands are high, these canonical features are necessary to capture attention and reduce IB.

Persuh and Melara (2016) demonstrated that participants could fail to notice a highly salient and familiar object – Barack Obama's face – when it appeared alone in the visual field. In their first experiment, participants engaged in a gender discrimination task involving faces presented peripherally. On the critical trial, a novel shape was presented centrally. Despite the lack of competing stimuli, 50 per cent of participants failed to notice the novel shape. In a subsequent experiment, the researchers presented the face of Barack Obama instead of a shape. Even though participants performed an easier task of colour discrimination, 60 per cent still failed to notice Obama's face. This phenomenon underscores the profound effect of top-down processes, such as expectation, on visual awareness and suggests that even a single, highly familiar object may not be perceived without attention.

In summary, the evidence from classical and recent studies reveals several key findings in IB research: attention is crucial for conscious perception, as demonstrated by the high rates of IB when attention is engaged in another task, and the similarity of unexpected objects to attended or ignored items significantly influences noticing rates, with greater similarity to ignored items leading to higher rates of IB.

Inattentional Blindness or Inattentional Amnesia?

Some have argued that IB reflects not a failure of conscious perception but of memory (Wolfe, 1999), suggesting that stimuli are consciously perceived but quickly forgotten, termed inattentional amnesia. Ward and Scholl (2015) conducted experiments to determine if IB is due to perceptual or memory failures, employing a novel method to induce repeated IB within the same session.

In the first experiment, participants counted how many times shapes crossed a midline on a screen while a grey cross (the unexpected event) appeared. After this, participants were told to watch for unexpected events. Despite this instruction, many missed a new unexpected event (a black 'E'). Specifically, 29 per cent of those who missed the initial grey cross also missed the black 'E', even though they were required to report immediately after its appearance. This suggested that IB is due to perceptual limitations rather than memory failures. In the second experiment, participants were instructed to immediately report any unexpected events, with coloured shapes introduced to enhance salience. Thirteen per cent of participants failed to notice a novel unexpected event despite the immediate reporting requirement. These findings reinforced that IB is not due to a failure to encode visual information into memory but rather a genuine deficit in moment-by-moment conscious perception.

Earlier support for IB being a perceptual and not a memory process comes from an fMRI study by Rees et al. (1999). This study challenged the idea that word processing occurs automatically, regardless of attention. The researchers observed robust left-hemisphere brain activations when participants attended to a stream of letters and words, specifically when processing meaningful words compared to random consonant strings. This indicated that the brain distinguishes between words and non-words when attention is directed towards the letter stream. However, when participants focused on a different visual task, such as attending to pictures, the same meaningful words no longer activated the brain areas previously engaged during the attended condition. There was no significant brain activation for words compared to consonant strings in the unattended condition. This absence of differential brain activity suggests that word processing is not automatic and requires attention for semantic processing to occur. Collectively, these findings support IB as a failure of perception rather than a failure to remember the seen stimuli.

Change Blindness

Another phenomenon that illustrates the importance of attention in conscious perception is change blindness (CB), the failure of observers to notice large changes in images when there is some visual disruption, such as a blink, a saccadic eye movement, a 'mud splash', or brief presentations of the scenes interspersed with blank intervals (Rensink et al., 1997; Simons & Levin, 1997; Simons & Rensink, 2005). For example, Rensink et al. (1997) presented a scene for 240 ms, followed by a blank inter-stimulus interval (ISI) of 80 ms. This was followed by the same scene (240 ms) with a change to an item in the scene. The participant's task was to detect and report the change. These alternations continued until they did so. In one demonstration, an engine of an aeroplane in the centre of the image alternated between appearing and disappearing.

The researchers found that participants typically take many alternations to notice the change, with changes of central interest, such as the main object in a scene, being noticed more quickly than changes of marginal interest, such as background details or minor objects. Attention is shown to be key, as it is necessary for detecting changes: when the item of change is attended, the change is noticed quickly; when it is not, the change can go unnoticed for several cycles of alternation. This suggests that without attention, significant changes in the visual field are not consciously perceived (Rensink et al., 1997).

However, it is important to note that these results do not provide evidence that the pre-change object was not consciously perceived before the change occurred. It is possible that the object was consciously perceived but that this representation was overwritten by the post-change scene (Becker & Anstis, 2000; Clarke & Mack, 2015). Therefore, CB is not the same as IB (Jensen et al., 2011). In IB experiments, participants are not expecting anything else to appear, whereas in CB, they are. Not noticing a change without attention is not the same as not noticing the pre-change object without attention.

Attentional Blink

Another phenomenon demonstrating the necessity of attention for conscious perception is the attentional blink (AB). In a typical rapid serial visual presentation (RSVP) experiment, participants detect two target stimuli (e.g., letters) presented in a rapid sequence of distractors (digits), each displayed for 100 milliseconds (Raymond et al., 1992). Researchers manipulate the temporal distance (lag) between the first (T1) and second target (T2) to study its effect on T2 detection rates. If T2 appears within 200–500 milliseconds after T1, participants often fail to detect it despite successfully detecting T1. This interval is known as the 'attentional blink' period, during which the attentional system is momentarily overloaded with processing T1, limiting resources for processing T2 effectively.

Recent studies have further explored the neural and cognitive mechanisms underlying the AB. Martens and Wyble (2010) reviewed evidence suggesting that the AB results from both temporary suppression of attention and competition between targets for limited processing resources. The 'boost and bounce' model by Olivers and Meeter (2008) posits that the first target 'boosts' attentional resources, followed by a 'bounce' or suppression phase, hindering subsequent stimuli processing.

In an ERP study, Revonsuo and Koivisto (2008) found that AB and repetition blindness (RB) reflect early perceptual deficits rather than being purely post-perceptual or memory-related phenomena. They observed that the ERP components associated with consciously recognized targets diverge from those associated with unrecognized targets as early as 250 ms after stimulus onset, indicating that both AB and RB involve impairments in conscious perception at an early stage.

Sergent and Dehaene (2004) provide evidence against 'residual' consciousness during the AB. They found an all-or-none pattern of T2 perception: participants either saw T2 clearly or not at all, with minimal intermediate visibility ratings. This bimodal distribution indicates that T2 either reaches full conscious awareness or remains entirely non-conscious during the AB period. Furthermore, the absence of neural markers associated with conscious perception, such as the P3b component, when T2 is not reported, reinforces the notion that T2 does not reach conscious experience in a degraded form. Thus, the evidence suggests no 'residual' conscious experience of T2 during the AB, but an absence of conscious perception due to attentional limitations (Sergent & Dehaene, 2004; Sergent et al., 2005).

This interpretation is supported by a study investigating neural processing differences between conscious and nonconscious processing during the AB

(Sergent et al., 2005). The study utilized ERPs to examine the brain's temporal dynamics in processing visual targets. It found that early visual ERP components (P1 and N1) were present regardless of T2 visibility, indicating these components do not correlate with conscious perception. The critical difference emerged around 270 ms post-stimulus, where ERPs for seen and unseen T2s diverged, with later components like N2, N3, P3a, and P3b appearing only when T2 was consciously perceived. This suggests that conscious access involves late-stage processing within a distributed cortical network. However, this interpretation may need updating given a recent ERP study by Cohen et al. (2020), who found P3b in a report condition but an absence of this proposed signature of conscious perception in the no-report condition. These findings suggest that the P3b is associated with the report of the stimulus rather than awareness of it, which the evidence showed participants are, in both the report and the no-report conditions.

It should be noted that there is some debate regarding the mechanisms underlying the AB, with some theorists proposing that attentional limitation is the causal factor (Raffone et al., 2014; Raymond et al., 1992), and others that the AB is due to working memory limitations (Chun & Potter, 1995; Jolicoeur & Dell'Acqua, 1998). A recent review of the ERP research on the AB (Zivony & Lamy, 2022) suggests that both attentional engagement and working memory encoding disruptions contribute. Their findings indicate that the failure to report T2 is often associated with a reduced and delayed N2pc component, signifying impaired attentional engagement, as well as a diminished P3 component, reflecting compromised working memory encoding. This suggests that the AB emerges from a combination of these factors, rather than being solely a limitation of either.

Retroactive Induction of Conscious Perception

In another study, attention was shown to retroactively induce conscious perception of a no-longer-present stimulus (Sergent et al., 2013). While this study does not explicitly show the necessity of attention for consciousness, it demonstrates that stimuli which can otherwise go unnoticed are consciously experienced when attended to. The test stimulus was a single Gabor patch of random orientation that could be flashed randomly within one of two circles positioned to the left or right of fixation. A Gabor patch is a visual stimulus used in vision research, consisting of sinusoidal wave grating, usually seen as alternating light and dark bars or stripes, which are used to study visual processing. The participant's task was to report the orientation of the patch. The target contrast at which each participant could determine the orientation of the patch with 80 per cent accuracy without cueing was determined first. During the experiment, attention was randomly cued to the left, right, or both circles by dimming the circle. The dimming could occur either before (200 ms) or after (up to 400 ms) the presentation of the Gabor patch.

The main finding was that post-cueing up to 400 ms after the disappearance of the target significantly improved accuracy in the orientation task compared to the 80 per cent accuracy in the absence of the cue. While bilateral post-cueing improved orientation discrimination up to 200 ms after the target (and thus, the effect could be due to the effects of post-cueing per se rather than attention), at 400 ms after the target, the bilateral effect disappeared, and only the congruent post-cue (i.e., when the target and cue appeared in the exact location) produced an improvement in orientation discrimination. Having ruled out that the effect was due to a kind of 'blindsight' – a phenomenon where individuals with lesions in their striate cortex can respond to visual stimuli without conscious perception – and not conscious perception of the stimulus by showing that visibility ratings positively correlated with objective performance, the researchers concluded that post-cueing attention can retroactively cause the conscious perception of a stimulus.

4.3.2 Evidence That Attention Is Not Required for Conscious Perception

We now turn to findings which have been claimed to be evidence of conscious perception without attention.

First, findings from behavioural experiments suggest that gist perception can occur in the absence or near-absence of attention. Li et al. (2002) conducted a study where participants performed a difficult task at the centre of the screen (reporting whether an array of 'L's contains a 'T') while a scene containing an animal or a vehicle was briefly presented in the visual periphery. The results showed that participants could detect whether the peripheral scene contained an animal or a vehicle without the performance of the central task suffering significantly. If attention were required for gist perception, one would predict a decline in central task performance. The fact that it did not suggests that gist perception can occur with minimal attention. This finding has been cited as an example of conscious perception without attention (Koch, 2007).

Iconic Memory (IM)

Second, IM has been proposed as an example of attention-free awareness (Block, 2007; Lamme, 2003). Iconic memory is a brief visual store that retains a high-fidelity representation of the visual scene for a short duration (around 300 ms) after the offset of the visual stimulus. In a series of classic experiments,

George Sperling (1960) investigated how much information human observers can perceive in a single brief exposure to a stimulus. He confirmed that the well-established span of immediate memory – what participants could report seeing after a briefly presented (50 ms) grid of alphanumeric characters – was limited to three to four letters. This finding was consistent regardless of the array type (e.g., different numbers or arrangements of the letters on the screen) or the presentation time (ranging from 50 ms to 500 ms). However, participants consistently reported that they perceived more than they could report.

Reasoning that the limitation lay with memory (only three to four items) and not visual experience, Sperling devised an ingenious way to circumvent this. He required participants to report a randomly selected subset of the letters in the grid (a partial report versus the whole report described in the previous paragraph). By requiring report of only one of the three rows of three to four letters (top, middle, or bottom row) of the grid, which was randomly cued by a high, medium, or low tone immediately after the display offset, Sperling found that participants could report all or most of the items in that row, no matter which row was randomly cued. Based on this, he reasoned that they must have information about the whole array available at the offset of the display, as they could access the information from any row when cued immediately.

Furthermore, by delaying the time between the display offset and cue onset, he found that the information about the display available to the participant decayed rapidly as a function of time. Participants reported fewer and fewer letters from any cued row, such that around 300 ms, the partial-report performance was no different from the whole-report. Sperling reasoned that after the display offset, a visual store exists in which all information is momentarily available, but which decays rapidly (around 300 ms). This was called iconic memory (Coltheart, 1980; Neisser, 1967).

IM has been extensively studied since Sperling's pioneering work in 1960. Researchers have built upon his findings, exploring different aspects and types of sensory memory (Averbach & Coriell, 1961; Becker et al., 2000; Clarke & Mack, 2015; Coltheart, 1980; Sligte et al., 2010). Different kinds of information persist for different durations in sensory memory, leading to distinctions such as informational persistence and visible persistence. Informational persistence relates to the ability to extract information from a briefly presented visual stimulus, while visible persistence refers to the continuation of a visual sensation after stimulus offset (Coltheart & Coltheart, 2010).

More recently, in experiments exploring IM using a change detection paradigm, in which one item, a rectangle in an array of rectangles in a notional circle, changes orientation after a brief inter-stimulus interval, the general finding is that participants can detect four to five items for change (Landman et al., 2003;

also see Becker et al. (2000)) without a cue. However, if after the offset of the first array, a cue directs attention to the to-be-changed item before the onset of the second array, participants perform significantly better, suggesting that they are using an IM of the first array to identify the orientation of that cued rectangle and comparing that information with the orientation of the rectangle in the second array (see also Clarke & Mack 2015).

In another study using the change-detection paradigm to explore the nature of non-attended representations, Vandenbroucke et al. (2012) found that so-called non-attended items in IM contain hallmarks that they have been consciously processed, namely perceptual inference, in which our perceptions deviate from the physical stimulus, for example, illusory contours. Using the Kanizsa triangle illusion, the investigators found the presence of these illusory shapes in IM. Importantly, the effect disappeared when the inducers were made isoluminant with the background, thus reducing the phenomenal effect and the illusion. If participants were relying on some cognitive (i.e., inferring the presence of a triangle) rather than perceptual (i.e., actually experiencing the illusory tri-angle) interpretation of the display for their report, then they should do just as well in the isoluminant condition as in the illusion-inducing condition. As they did not, the authors concluded that they must have been basing their report on phenomenal rather than unconscious representations.

Many investigators (e.g., Block, Lamme, Koch – those who argue that attention is not necessary for consciousness) explain the Vandenbroucke et al., Landman et al., and Sperling phenomena as follows: when a visual display is presented, we can only focally attend to around four or five of the items in the display, but when cued, we can report any of the items in the display. In addition, participants report they can see the whole array. Therefore, if the amount of items that can be consciously reported exceeds the number of items that can be attended, it follows that more can be seen than can be attended, and so attention is not a precondition for consciousness. In other words, we can only attend to four or five items, but we are conscious of more than can be attended (if cued, we can report any row of the 3 × 4 matrix of letters in the Sperling experiments); therefore, attention is not necessary for consciousness.

A recent experiment seems to lend this strong support. In an attempt to explore the sensitivity of observers to phenomenal colour information outside the focus of attention (with the hypothesis that for a fleeting moment, rich colour information is ephemerally experienced outside focal attention and rapidly becomes unavailable for report), Bronfman et al. (2014) looked for evidence of a summary statistic, colour diversity (high diversity or low diversity of colours in the display), which necessitates differentiation between individual colours in the display. Compressing information about the individual colours into a binary low colour diversity/high colour diversity variable creates this summary statistic. This is stored while the information about the individual colours themselves decays. Using a Sperling-like array of rows of coloured letters, the researchers first pre-cued the location of the row. The cue was a white rectangle appearing against a black background. The twenty-four-letter array then appeared for 300 ms followed by a 900 ms blank interval and a white square appearing at the location of one of the letters in the pre-cued row. The participant's task initially was to report the cued letter (a measure of working memory capacity), but after completing experimental blocks with letter report alone, participants repeated the letter report task along with the additional task of assessing the colour diversity of the cued or uncued rows.

The overall finding was that working memory capacity for the letters was not significantly reduced when participants had the additional colour diversity task to perform. Furthermore, sensitivity to colour diversity was significantly above chance, and this sensitivity was the same for the colour content of cued rows as it was for uncued rows. After ruling out the possibility that the colour diversity performance was supported by subliminal perception of the colour information in the uncued rows (participants could not do the colour diversity task when coloured masks rendered the target colours invisible), and ruling out the possibility that it was due to trial-by-trial shifts of attention (attending to colour on some trials and letters on another), the authors concluded that these experiments provide evidence that non-attended information (here, colour diversity) is consciously experienced. If it were not, they reasoned, colour diversity judgements should be able to occur under conditions where the target is made invisible by masking (subliminal perception), and their results do not support this. Instead, they argue, non-attended representations have a rich perceptual nature.

ERP Evidence for Attention-Free Consciousness?

Further evidence for the independence of consciousness from attention comes from even ERP studies. ERPs are invaluable tools for investigating the temporal dynamics of visual consciousness allowing researchers to delineate the sequence of neural events associated with the unconscious and conscious processing of visual stimuli. This method enables examining the relationship between attention and consciousness by observing the temporal order of ERP components related to each process. If a reliable marker of conscious perception of the stimulus is seen before one of attention, then this would suggest the former is independent of the latter.

The earliest reliable activity related to subjective visual awareness of a stimulus is the visual awareness negativity (VAN), characterized by a negative amplitude difference in posterior brain areas around 200 ms following stimulus onset

(Forster et al., 2020). This has been supported by various studies, evincing VAN as a crucial neural marker for conscious visual perception (Eklund & Wiens, 2018; Jiminez et al., 2021; Koivisto & Revonsuo, 2010; Railo, Koivisto, & Revonsuo, 2011). Some studies indicate that the onset of VAN can occur slightly earlier, around 100 ms, but generally peaks between 200 and 250 ms (Koivisto et al., 2009; Railo et al., 2011). This conscious processing signature is seen under many experimental conditions (e.g., binocular rivalry, CB, masking, AB) and has been reported to be independent of selective attention (Koivisto & Revonsuo, 2010; Railo et al., 2011). It is typically followed by a late positive amplitude (LP) in parietal areas around 400 ms after stimulus onset. Due to different latencies, polarities, and scalp locations, different aspects of consciousness are assumed to underlie these two processes. Some researchers (Koivisto et al., 2009) propose that the VAN reflects phenomenal consciousness (the subjective visual impression of seeing something), while the LP reflects reflective or access consciousness (a visual experience that can be reported, rehearsed in working memory, categorized, and acted upon).

In an experiment designed to examine the effects of non-spatial attention on visual awareness, Koivisto et al. (2008) presented a grey dot near the subjective threshold while measuring ERPs averaged for conscious detection of the stimuli and non-detections separately. The investigators found evidence of a VAN around 180–350 ms after stimulus onset at occipital and posterior temporal locations for awareness of the dot compared to no awareness of the dot. As predicted, this VAN was followed by an LP after 400–500 ms, peaking in parietal areas. Importantly, they found that this activity (the VAN and LP) was unaffected when attention was manipulated. To manipulate attention to the stimulus (the grey dot), the inter-stimulus interval between the offset of the fixation cross and the onset of the dot was either constant and predictable or varied unpredictably. By doing this, they assumed that attention in the unpredictable condition would not be as well controlled as in the constant (predictable onset) condition. Therefore, if attention played a role in VAN, there would be an ERP difference between the predictable and unpredictable onset conditions. However, there was no significant difference, suggesting that this early correlate of visual consciousness is not dependent on non-spatial attention.

In another study, Koivisto and Revonsuo (2007) manipulated spatial attention and non-spatial selection of targets. Participants attended to visual targets while ignoring non-targets in the prespecified visual field and all stimuli in the opposite field. Visual consciousness was manipulated by masking. The target stimulus was presented for 17 ms, followed by a blank screen (17 ms), and then masked (17 ms). They found that the VAN was independent of non-spatial selection, replicating earlier studies, while the LP component depended on it.

Furthermore, spatial attention did not affect VAN but did affect LP, as shown by enhanced electrophysiological activity with spatial attention. They concluded that phenomenal visual awareness is not reliant on spatial or non-spatial attention, whereas access or reflective consciousness is.

Taken together, this evidence supports the notion that conscious perception can occur without attention. Gist perception experiments demonstrate that participants can recognize scenes with minimal attention. IM studies reveal that brief visual storage of high-fidelity images does not require focused attention. Finally, ERP studies indicate that neural correlates of conscious perception can be observed even when attention is not directed at the stimuli. These findings challenge the view that attention is a prerequisite for conscious perception. How can these findings be reconciled with the evidence discussed earlier?

4.3.3 Challenging the Assumption of Attention-Free Conscious Perception

It is crucial to question the assumption that participants' performance in these experiments is based on unattended information. In IM experiments, participants are instructed to attend to the screen since changes could occur in any item of the eight-item circle display (as in Landman et al.'s experiments) or in any of the rows of the 3×4 matrix (as in Sperling's experiments). This scenario involves attention, not attention-free processing, as participants are expecting changes or cues in specific items.

Similarly, in visual pop-out experiments – where participants must identify a target among distractors, such as a green circle among red circles – and tasks where participants are engaged in a primary task but expecting a secondary task, participants are actively attending to stimuli. These experiments do not measure preattentive vision because participants are actively attending and expecting targets. For instance, Treisman and Gelade (1980) found that increasing the number of distractors did not increase detection time, suggesting that the targets were processed preattentively, perceptually 'popping out' without focused attention. However, detecting targets with conjunctions of features required attention, as detection time increased with more distractors.

Mack and Rock (1998) and Pitts et al. (2018) argue that such methods used to study preattentive vision do not provide evidence of conscious perception without attention. Mack and Rock state:

> Prior research into the relation between perception and attention has been based on a method that not only fails to eliminate attention, but in fact depends upon it. ... In every case, the observers are engaging in a visual

search, which by definition requires attention. To look and try to find something is to attend to the array in which it might be present and intend to see it. How then can one conclude that attention has been eliminated? (Mack & Rock, 1998, p. 5)

These methods fail to dissociate the effects of attention and expectation. What Mack and Rock describe can be termed 'Expectant Attention': participants are both attending to the task and expecting stimuli to appear. This is in contrast to IB experiments, where participants are not expecting the stimulus, making IB paradigms (IB) better for studying attention without expectation. In these conditions, when participants are focused on one task and an unexpected stimulus is presented, they typically do not report conscious perception of the stimulus.

Supporting this, Hsieh et al. (2011) found that participants presented with a feature singleton among homogeneous distractors, with their awareness suppressed by continuous flash suppression, performed better on an orientation–discrimination task at the location of the unseen feature singleton compared to a control location. This indicates that a feature singleton can capture attention without awareness. However, when attention was diverted by a demanding task, this subliminal pop-out effect disappeared. These findings suggest that low-level visual features can attract attention without awareness, but top-down attention is crucial for this effect, challenging theories proposing preattentive processing of such features.

In an attempt to explore whether attention is required for IM, Mack et al. (2015) manipulated attention to a Sperling-like matrix presented at fixation by varying the probability that the matrix's contents would be reported or a judgement about the similarity of four circles in the visual periphery would be required. The probability of reporting either the circle or the matrix was manipulated, as was the difficulty of the circle task.

The matrix stimuli consisted of six letters arranged in a 3 × 2 grid, centred at fixation. The entire matrix was visible for 250 ms. For the matrix task, a cue appeared immediately after the array offset. Two horizontal lines, one blue and one black, indicated the row participants needed to report. The lines were visible for 500 ms, followed by a prompt to enter the letters. The circle stimuli involved four circles positioned at the corners of an imaginary square around the matrix. In the easy visual search condition, the circles were either all red or all green, or one was an odd colour among the others. In the hard search condition, the circles were vertically bisected with different colours on each half. An auditory 1500 Hz tone signalled the start of the circle task. Participants responded by pressing 's' for same and 'd' for different to indicate whether the circles were the same or different. Both matrix and circle stimuli were presented in each array.

Attention was manipulated in two ways: by combining the report of letters with either an easy or a hard search task (within-subject manipulation) and by varying the probability of which of the two tasks (matrix or circle) was cued (between-subject manipulation). In the within-subject condition, participants performed both tasks in dual-task conditions, with cues indicating the task to perform immediately after array offset. In the between-subject condition, the probability of performing either the matrix or circle task varied across trials (40/60, 60/40, 80/20), with ten participants tested in each condition. Participants first completed sixty trials of each control condition before the dual tasks. The control conditions included a single easy circle task, a single hard circle task, and a single matrix task. Following this, participants completed 100 trials for each dual-task condition, combining the matrix task with an easy or hard circle search task.

The researchers found that the number of letters reported from the matrix decreased significantly when participants' attention was diverted to the circle task, especially when the circle task was difficult, and the probability of performing the matrix task was low. In the partial report condition, the number of letters reported was significantly greater when the matrix task was the only task compared to when it was paired with either the easy or hard circle task. In the whole report condition, a similar trend was observed: matrix task performance was significantly better when it was the only task compared to when it was paired with the circle tasks. This decrease in performance with increased attentional load suggests that attention is required for the formation and retrieval of information from IM.

Moreover, in a follow-up study (Mack et al., 2016) to test whether participants had some phenomenal awareness of the matrix's presence on the screen despite not being able to report its specific contents, the researchers further manipulated the probability of reporting the letters in the matrix. Participants were again presented with a Sperling-like matrix of letters alongside a set of circles, and task cues were given immediately after the stimulus array disappeared. However, this time, the probability of performing the matrix task was reduced to only 10 per cent, with the remaining 90 per cent of trials dedicated to the circle task.

Participants completed 101 trials in this experiment, with the critical 101st trial designed to assess their awareness. No matrix was presented at all on the critical trial. Instead, participants were cued to perform the circle task, but immediately after the cue, they were asked to enter the letters from the matrix. If they entered letters and reported not noticing anything different, they were considered to be inattentionally blind to the absence of the matrix. In contrast, the control condition had participants cued to the matrix task in 90 per cent of the trials and the circle task in the remaining 10 per cent. In the critical trial in the control condition, the matrix was also absent, and participants were asked to enter the letters.

The results were striking: eight out of the fifteen participants (53 per cent) in the experimental condition were unaware that the matrix was absent and entered letters into the response box. In contrast, all ten participants in the control condition (100 per cent) were aware of the absence of the matrix. To ensure that the participants unaware of the matrix's absence were not simply disengaged from the task, the researchers compared the circle task performance of aware and unaware participants on the last ten trials before the critical trial. Both groups performed similarly on the circle task, indicating that the lack of awareness was not due to disengagement.

A follow-up experiment further investigated this by presenting a matrix where each letter was flipped horizontally and vertically on the 101st trial. Here, seven out of ten participants (70 per cent) in the experimental condition were unaware of the reorientation, while all six control participants noticed the change, reinforcing the findings from the first experiment.

Supporting these findings, Otten et al. (2023) recently demonstrated the susceptibility of both IM and short-term memory (STM) to expectation-driven illusions. In their series of experiments, participants viewed memory displays containing six to eight letters arranged around fixation (the centre of the screen), in a notional clock-face configuration. The displays contained both real and pseudo-letters (mirrored letters, 'ɔ' for 'C'), were presented briefly for 250 ms, and were masked. Despite attention being focused on the task, participants often reported high-confidence errors, recalling letters that were never actually presented. Memory tests conducted after retention intervals of 0.75 seconds, 3 seconds, and under conditions with interference revealed significant memory distortions. These high-confidence errors increased over time, indicating that as memory decayed, expectations increasingly distorted their STM content. This study demonstrates that expectations can significantly influence different stages of short-term memory even when attention is actively engaged.

Another study used a combination of the Bronfman et al. paradigm and the Mack & Rock IB paradigm to examine whether summary statistics like colour diversity and size diversity would be seen under conditions of inattention; that is, when the participant does not expect anything other than the letter task to occur (Jackson-Nielson et al., 2015). If attention is not required for colour diversity perception (as Bronfman et al. appear to demonstrate), then colour diversity perception should occur under these conditions of inattention. In these experiments, participants performed the Bronfman et al. working memory coloured letter task on several non-critical trials. On the critical trial, the colour diversity of the uncued rows changed from low to high (or vice versa), or the diversity of the size of the letters changed from low to high (or vice versa). The finding was that across all experiments, more than 50 per cent of participants were inattentionally blind to the colour and size statistics of the uncued rows on the critical trial (they could not reliably pick out the display they had just seen from a three-alternative forced-choice array). This is in stark contrast to the findings of Bronfman et al. From the results of the Jackson-Nielson and Pitts study, it seems that when attention is suitably taxed, little to nothing of the non-attended stimuli are seen.

Finally, while early ERP studies seemed to confirm the independence of visual consciousness from attention (Koivisto & Revonsuo, 2005; Koivisto & Revonsuo, 2007; Koivisto et al., 2005), the authors themselves advised caution (Koivisto & Revonsuo, 2009) in interpreting their results this way. In Koivisto and Revonsuo's (2007) study, unilateral stimuli were used, creating the possibility that rapid attentional shifts could occur between the attended blank field and the unattended field (where a target might appear). Suppose this is the case, and the effect (a VAN) is removed when a stricter manipulation suitably controls spatial attention. In that case, the VAN is not independent of spatial attention.

In a subsequent experiment to test this hypothesis, Koivisto et al. (2009) presented two letter stimuli bilaterally at spatially distinct locations, requiring participants to attend to one location (thus effectively ignoring the other). Using this method with bilateral stimuli, the researchers could measure the effects of spatial attention more accurately. In this experiment, two different letter stimuli were presented simultaneously for 17 ms, one in each visual field. This was followed by a 17 ms blank period; then the first mask was presented for 17 ms, making the stimuli invisible in masked conditions. The first mask was presented in only one visual field for unmasked conditions, leaving the other field's stimulus visible. The second mask was followed after a blank period of 84 ms and presented for 17 ms. The stimulus-mask SOA was 33 ms for masked and 133 ms for unmasked conditions. Participants were instructed to detect and respond to target letters in the attended field while ignoring the unattended field. Six blocks of trials were conducted, with attention alternated between visual fields.

The results for the attended field replicated earlier findings, showing that the VAN occurs around 130–300 ms after stimulus onset. However, no VAN was observed for stimuli presented in the unattended location, indicating that spatial attention is necessary for the emergence of conscious perception and that unintentional attentional shifts towards the target stimulus may have influenced previous results. The study also found that while the VAN depends on spatial attention, the late positivity (LP) component, which occurs around 400–500 ms post-stimulus, reflects later stages of cognitive processing and is influenced by both spatial and non-spatial attention. This distinction suggests that phenomenal visual awareness (indexed by VAN) requires spatial attention, whereas reflective consciousness (indexed by LP) involves both types of attention.

Shafto and Pitts (2015) found evidence that VAN was not present during IB. In their study, they used a modified IB paradigm where participants were initially unaware of face stimuli due to a demanding distracter task. The study involved three phases: during the first phase, participants performed a distracter task and were subsequently assessed for awareness of faces. Those who reported no awareness of the faces were considered inattentionally blind. In the second phase, the same distracter task was performed, but participants were now aware of the face stimuli. In the third phase, participants focused on a discrimination task involving the faces. The results showed that the N170 (a marker of face perception) and VAN were absent during IB (Phase 1) and present when participants were aware of the faces (Phases 2 and 3). This suggests that both the N170 and VAN are modulated by attention and awareness, indicating that conscious face perception involves these early-to-mid latency neural responses, which are disrupted during IB. Using the same IB paradigm with words as the stimulus, Schelonka et al. (2017) found similar results, namely an absence of VAN when participants were not aware of the stimulus.

More recently, Harris et al. (2020) conducted a no-report IB study that provides some strong evidence linking visual awareness with attention. Their study specifically explored the relationship between post-stimulus alpha power and awareness using ERPs. Alpha oscillations, which are brain waves in the frequency range of 8–14 Hz, are known to be involved in various cognitive processes, including attention and sensory processing. The researchers found that VAN was only present when participants were aware of the stimuli. Conversely, VAN was absent during inattention, where participants did not consciously perceive the stimuli. This indicates that VAN is a neural marker of awareness and is absent when attention is not directed towards the stimulus, leading to IB. The study involved forty-eight participants, divided into two groups: an IB group and a control group. Participants engaged in a target discrimination task, with irrelevant, non-salient shape probes presented peripherally. The control group was informed about these probes, while the IB group was not made aware until halfway through the experiment. The study revealed that when participants were aware of the probes, there was a significant reduction in post-stimulus alpha power contralateral to the stimulus. This reduction in alpha power did not occur when the stimulus was not perceived, further demonstrating the role of attention in facilitating conscious awareness. The absence of alpha-power reduction in IB conditions underscores the necessity of attention for visual consciousness.

In an even more recent study, Doradzińska and Bola (2021) investigated the Perceptual Awareness Negativity (PAN), a signature of generalized perceptual awareness occurring around 120–200 ms following the offset of the stimulus (Dembski et al., 2021), and its relationship with attention. They reanalysed data from a previously published experiment where awareness and attention were orthogonally manipulated using backward-masked and unmasked stimuli that were either task-relevant or irrelevant. The findings indicated that PAN is highly dependent on both exogenous (stimulus saliency) and endogenous attention (task relevance). The early time window of PAN (140–200 ms) showed that PAN was only present when stimuli were task-relevant, disappearing when they were task-irrelevant. This suggests that early PAN is not independent of attention. In the late time window (200–350 ms), PAN was modulated by stimulus saliency, with fearful faces eliciting stronger PAN responses than neutral faces. These results challenge the notion of PAN as an attention-independent marker of awareness, showing that it is closely tied to attentional processes (Bola & Doradzińska, 2021).

Finally, Ciupińska et al. (2024), in what may seem to be counter-evidence, found that VAN was independent of two attentional mechanisms, namely temporal cueing and spatiotemporal orienting. Using a Posner cueing paradigm along with measuring ERPs, they found that VAN occurred with and without attention, suggesting that phenomenal consciousness can occur in the absence of attention. However, the same argument can be applied to this interpretation as was expressed earlier: participants are giving some attention to both locations on the screen and are expecting a stimulus to appear. This study used a method where participants were engaged in a task requiring them to detect and identify a Gabor patch stimulus, inherently involving attention. Therefore, as the researchers themselves acknowledge, the method used does not eliminate attention. This is another instance of Mack and Rock's (1998) critique of experimental methods used to measure perception without attention, where the experimental setup itself requires participants to engage in visual search and attend to potential target locations. Thus, it cannot conclusively demonstrate conscious perception without attention.

While the debate continues and remains open to future investigation, the weight of evidence strongly supports the notion of some form of attentional mechanism being required for conscious perception. In all cases where it is claimed that conscious perception of some target has occurred without attention (e.g., gist perception and IM), it is found that participants are indeed attending. They attend to the screen to perform the required task, expect to see the targets, and intend to do it. As described earlier in this section, a more precise characterization of what participants do in such experiments reveals that their actions cannot be described as inattention. Indeed, when attention is heavily taxed by a difficult task (leading to inattention to a target), conscious perception of the gist of a scene is not found, nor is IM.

In the next sections, we explore the effects of expectation as well as the interplay between attention and expectation on visual perception and detail some experiments which revealed a surprising and intriguing result. While we found evidence that attention is necessary for IM as described earlier, we also found that under conditions of inattention and with an experimentally created expectation, participants reported what they expected to see in the unattended location. These findings suggest that while attention is necessary for conscious perception, a strong expectation that a stimulus will appear can lead to an illusory conscious perception of the expected stimulus when selective attention is elsewhere – a phenomenon we term 'Expectation Awareness'. To put it simply, expectation alone can generate an experience independently of attention.

5 Expectation

5.1 Expectation and Perception

Expectations are predictions that the brain generates based on prior knowledge, contextual cues and past experiences about the noisy, ambiguous sensory input (Kok et al., 2013; Series & Seitz, 2013; Summerfield & de Lange, 2014). These predictions streamline cognitive processing by establishing mental frameworks that filter and prioritize information, enhancing our ability to navigate the physical and social environment. Extensive research has shown that expectations play a crucial role in various aspects of perception. For instance, expectations affect motion perception, leading to more accurate and faster responses to expected motion directions (Alink et al., 2010; Kveraga et al., 2007). Similarly, expectations influence colour perception, making us perceive colours closer to what we predict (Olkkonen et al., 2008; Witzel & Gegenfurtner, 2013). Other visual features, such as contrast and brightness, are shaped by expectations, demonstrating the extensive impact of predictive mechanisms on perception (see Summerfield & de Lange (2014) for a review).

5.2 Structural and Contextual Expectations

Expectations can be categorized into structural and contextual types (Series & Seitz, 2013). Structural expectations are formed through long-term interactions with the environment and result from implicit learning of the statistical regularities of the world around us. For example, consider the circles with light and dark shading in Figure 6. Circles with light at the top appear convex, while those with dark at the top look concave. This phenomenon occurs because the visual system assumes that light comes from above, an expectation based on everyday experiences with natural lighting (Bar, 2004). Structural expectations are the 'default' expectations of the information processing system and are either hardwired or based on implicit learning of the statistics of the natural environment (Series & Seitz, 2013).

Moreover, we have a bias towards recognizing cardinal orientations – up, down, left, and right – more accurately than oblique angles (Girshick et al., 2011). This orientation bias influences how we orient ourselves and navigate spaces, impacting everything from architectural design to the layout of digital interfaces. Another interesting structural expectation is the brain's tendency to perceive objects as convex and backgrounds as homogeneously coloured (Goldreich & Peterson, 2012), a heuristic bias that simplifies the variegated array of visual stimuli we encounter, allowing us to quickly discern objects from their surroundings.

Studies show that these structural priors are not entirely immutable and can be reshaped through experience. For instance, Adams et al. (2004) demonstrated that the 'light-from-above' prior could be altered through visual-haptic

Figure 6 The light from above assumption.

training. Participants exposed to specific lighting conditions adapted their internal representations of light direction, which generalized to other tasks, indicating that the prior is flexible and influenced by experiential learning. This research demonstrates the dynamic nature of perceptual systems, revealing how even deeply ingrained visual expectations can be modified through interaction with the environment.

Contextual expectations, on the other hand, are rapidly modifiable and can be influenced by instructions, sensory cues, or the context in which a stimulus is shown. Some of the earliest research on contextual expectations comes from experiments using bistable figures (Bugelski & Alampay, 1961). In these experiments, participants were shown bistable figures (e.g., the rat/man image). Before viewing them, some participants were primed with pictures or words related to one of the possible interpretations. The results indicated that expectations, driven by prior experiences of human faces or small mammals, determined what was perceived.

One way that expectations manifest is through context frames. These frames represent sets of expectations about the environment that are triggered rapidly by either global scene information or key objects within a scene (Bar, 2004). They are populated with prototypical information about a given context, including the identities and typical spatial arrangements of objects that frequently co-appear. This mechanism allows the brain to predict what it will likely encounter next in the visual field and facilitates quicker and more efficient responses. For instance, seeing a steering wheel triggers expectations for the positions of other car-related elements, like the dashboard, radio, and mirrors, based on a stereotypical understanding of car interiors. These expectations are dynamic and continuously updated based on ongoing sensory input. The rapid activation of context frames is essential for managing the vast amount of visual information the brain processes, enabling it to focus on anomalies or unexpected features by comparing incoming data against these frameworks. This is highly adaptive as it conserves cognitive and neural resources and enhances perceptual efficiency, allowing the system to avoid repeatedly analysing every aspect of a familiar scene (Bar, 2004; Bar & Ullman, 1996).

A classic study by Palmer (1975) demonstrated the effect of contextual expectations on perception, specifically how the perception of objects is influenced by the scenes in which they are embedded. In his experiments, participants were shown objects within appropriate contextual scenes (e.g., a toaster in a kitchen), inappropriate scenes (e.g., a printer in a kitchen), or no context. The results revealed that congruent objects (e.g., the toaster in the kitchen) were identified more quickly and accurately than incongruent objects (e.g., the printer in the kitchen).

In a series of experiments, Biederman et al. investigated the role of scene coherence on object detection (Biederman, 1982; Biederman et al., 1974). In one experiment, participants viewed coherent and jumbled scenes to determine which object occupied a given cued position immediately after the scene was presented. Results indicated that participants were more accurate at identifying objects in coherent scenes than in jumbled scenes, even when they knew what objects to look for and where to look. This suggested that jumbling primarily affected perceptual recognition rather than memory or response selection (Biederman et al., 1973). They then extended these findings by examining the time required to identify objects in coherent versus jumbled scenes (Biederman et al., 1974). Participants were given a picture of a target object before viewing the scene and were then asked to judge whether the target object was present. The results showed slower detection times for objects in jumbled scenes, especially when the target object was not present but likely to occur.

In another study, they explored the effects of disrupting five semantic and physical relations that define a coherent scene on object perception: the probability for an object to appear in the scene, the position of the object within the scene, the relative size of the object, whether it was supported or not, and whether it was occluded (Biederman, 1981; Biederman et al., 1982). By manipulating these relations, the researchers could measure their effect on object identification. For example, one would expect to see a fire hydrant in the street but not in a kitchen, which would be a violation of probability – the likelihood of that object appearing in that context. One would also expect to see a chair on the floor and not on the ceiling (a violation of the position relation), a cup smaller than a kitchen table and not the opposite (a size violation), a sofa resting on the ground and not floating in the air (a violation of support), and a wall becoming occluded as a cat moves past it, not for the wall to remain visible through the cat (a violation of occlusion). In one experiment (Biederman et al., 1982), participants viewed scenes (150 ms) in which a cued object was either congruent with the scene or not. They found that, except for the occlusion relation, participants were less accurate and slower in detecting cued objects when these semantic and physical relations were violated. Interestingly, detecting a non-violating stimulus was not affected by the presence of another object undergoing a violation within the scene. This shows the powerful influence of scene schema in the perception and identification of objects within a scene.

Further support comes from Davenport and Potter (2004), who found that an object was identified more quickly when presented with a related background (e.g., a priest in a church) compared to an unrelated background (e.g., a priest in a football stadium). In this study, objects in isolation were identified most quickly. However, when there was a background to the object, the meaning of the context and the gist of the scene significantly impacted the reaction time for participants to name the target. The results led the authors to conclude that objects are not processed independently of their surroundings but interact with the processing of the scene (see also Oliva & Torallba (2007)), such that visual processing of the object is influenced by the scene gist.

Munneke et al. (2013) examined whether the scene consistency effect on object recognition is influenced by focused attention. They used a location cueing method where participants were informed about the target object's location on some trials, allowing them to direct their attention accordingly. The study found that scene consistency effects were independent of spatial attention, occurring whether participants' focus was on the target or the background. This suggests that consistent scene contexts aid object recognition regardless of attention, likely driven by global scene properties or 'scene gist', which are processed with minimal attention.

Further insights come from neuroimaging studies examining the modulation of object representations by scene context. In one experiment, degraded images of objects were shown either in isolation or within congruent scenes, such as a helicopter in the sky. fMRI results indicated that the presence of a scene context enhanced the neural representations of these objects, making the activity patterns in the object–selective cortex resemble those evoked by intact objects more closely. This neural sharpening effect was correlated with concurrent activity in scene-selective areas, suggesting that scene context provides predictive signals that enhance object processing (Brandman & Peelen, 2017).

These findings collectively emphasize the influence of scene context on object perception. Scene context, or the gist of the scene, provides a predictive framework shaped by prior experiences and expectations to more accurately and efficiently identify and interact with the objects within it. According to the Spatial Envelope Model (Oliva & Torralba, 2006), a scene has its own 'shape': a gestalt formed by global properties, such as the degree of naturalness, openness, expansion, roughness, and ruggedness. A forest, for example, has a greater degree of naturalness than a city square. One would expect irregular shapes and the organic texture of the leaves and trees in the former. In contrast, one would expect more horizontal and vertical edges and more geometric manufactured shapes in the latter. Scene gist is thus seen as a statistical summary of the scene, one which can be rapidly determined by global properties and which influences perception of the objects within that scene (Hollingworth & Henderson, 1999; Potter et al., 2014).

The psychophysical and neuroimaging findings on scene and object perception can be explained through a predictive processing framework. Peelen et al. (2024) have developed such a model that emphasizes the bidirectional

influences between scene and object perception. In their model, visual processing pathways for objects and scenes operate in parallel, with object processing
focusing on detailed, high-resolution foveal input and scene processing on
larger-scale, low-resolution peripheral input. These pathways interact hierarchically, where higher levels generate predictions to guide lower-level computa-
tions. In this predictive processing model, scene and object information is
integrated through precision-weighted Bayesian inference. This means that
the brain combines multiple sources of information, each weighted by its
reliability, to form a coherent percept. For example, scene context, which is
typically more reliable, can strongly guide object recognition. This hierarchical
structure allows for efficient disambiguation of ambiguous sensory input, as
higher-level scene representations provide predictive signals that enhance the
neural representations of objects in object-selective areas and vice versa.

5.3 Neural Mechanisms of Expectation

Recent research is revealing the neural mechanisms underlying the influence of
expectations on sensory processing. For example, Kok et al. (2011) explored
how predictions influence processing in the primary visual cortex (V1). Using
fMRI and multivariate pattern analysis (MVPA), they demonstrated that perceptual expectation reduced neural response amplitude in V1 while improving
the specificity of stimulus representation. This suggests that the brain uses
expectations to sharpen sensory representations, facilitating efficient and accurate perception.

Kok et al. (2013) further investigated how top-down expectations bias sensory representations in the visual cortex. They found that expectations significantly influenced neural activity in early visual cortex areas such as V1, V2, and
V3. The direction of motion reconstructed from the BOLD signal was biased in
the direction predicted by auditory cues, demonstrating that expectations alter
perception and underlying neural representations.

In another study, Kok et al. (2014) examined how prior expectations shape
sensory representations in the primary visual cortex. Using fMRI, they showed
that expectation of a visual stimulus evokes a feature-specific pattern of activity
in V1 similar to that evoked by the actual stimulus. This pre-activation of
stimulus-specific patterns suggests that the brain uses prior knowledge to
prepare sensory areas for expected inputs, enhancing perceptual accuracy and
efficiency.

Egner et al. (2010) explored how expectation and surprise influence neural
responses in the fusiform face area (FFA). Their fMRI study showed that high
expectations for faces led to reduced neural responses when faces were presented,

whereas unexpected faces elicited stronger responses. This supports the predictive coding model, where neural responses are shaped by both the prediction and the prediction error.

These findings are supported by Bayesian theories which posit that perception is biased towards expectations to optimize veridicality, increasing the gain on expected relative to unexpected inputs. In contrast, so-called Cancellation theories argue that perception is geared more towards unexpected signals to optimize informativeness, by suppressing expected sensory activity (Press et al., 2020). The two-process model proposed by Press et al. (2020) resolves this paradox by suggesting that perception initially biases towards expected inputs to rapidly generate veridical experiences. However, when inputs significantly deviate from predictions, generating high levels of surprise, a secondary process boosts these unexpected inputs. As predicted by the model, some studies show that expected events are perceived more intensely 50 ms post-stimulus, with this bias inverting by 200 ms to unexpected events (Yon & Press, 2017). Further supporting this, EEG research on infants has observed initial enhanced processing of expected events, which later transitions to a preference for unexpected events (Kouider et al., 2015).

The neural mechanisms of expectation, as revealed by these research findings, add support to the brain as a dynamic prediction machine, continually refining its rich hierarchical representation of the world to navigate the uncertainties of the environment, where minimizing surprise or free energy is crucial (Friston, 2010). Expectations inform what we perceive in the present moment. What you are perceiving right *now* is constructed from higher-level expectations (say, about an independent spatio-temporal world, object permanence), perhaps hardwired or learned developmentally and resistant to being updated; mid-level expectations about the dynamics of the current environment, about the street you are driving along, how these cars are behaving, how these people are behaving, and what they will do next; and lower-level expectations about the ever-changing tapestry of sensory information, about edges, motion, shape, depth, texture, and colour. The result is a perception of the world, sculpted by the interplay between predictions at each level and precision-weighted prediction errors.

In the last two sections, we have examined the roles of attention and expectation in perception.

We have reviewed evidence demonstrating the necessity of attention for conscious perception and the powerful influence of expectation on what we perceive. In the next section, we will explore research on the relationship between attention and expectation.

6 Attention and Expectation

6.1 Introduction

As we have seen, attention and expectation play significant roles in shaping perceptual experiences, influencing how we process and interpret sensory information. This section explores studies that examine how attention and expectation interact.

6.2 Expectation Violations and Attention Capture

Some experiments conducted in our lab (Mack et al., 2017) were guided by critical questions about the role of expectation violations in capturing attention. Earlier research had revealed that incongruities within a scene can unconsciously capture attention, leading to awareness of the scene. Mudrik et al. (2011) conducted studies demonstrating that scenes depicting incongruent actions, such as a woman baking a chessboard instead of cookies, can slow responses to subsequent scenes, whether congruent or incongruent.

In one of their studies, they presented masked scenes of a person performing an action with either a congruent or an incongruent object (e.g., a man pouring coffee into a mug versus a roll of toilet paper). These were followed by briefly presented target scenes containing either a congruent or incongruent object, and participants were tasked with judging the congruency of these targets as quickly as possible. The study found that reaction times were longer when targets were preceded by scenes with incongruent objects, even though the scenes were masked and not consciously perceived. This suggests that the brain processes relationships between objects and their contexts outside of consciousness, requiring additional cognitive resources to resolve incongruities. The invisibility of the masked scenes was confirmed through subjective and objective measures, eliminating the possibility of partial awareness. These results indicate that incongruent elements within a scene can be processed unconsciously, affecting the processing speed of subsequent stimuli (Mudrik & Koch, 2013). Furthermore, in studies involving binocular rivalry, Mudrik et al. (2011) found that incongruent scenes escape perceptual suppression faster than congruent ones and dominate visual consciousness for longer durations. This suggests that the brain allocates more attentional resources to resolve these incongruities, which are difficult to integrate without conscious processing (Mudrik et al., 2011).

6.3 Experimenting with Scene Incongruity

Inspired by these results, Mack et al. (2017) conducted experiments using the same stimuli in Mudrik et al.'s (2011) experiments to investigate whether scene incongruity captures attention and leads to conscious perception under four conditions: inattention, full attention, change detection, and IM.

In the first experiment, participants were exposed to scenes with congruent or incongruent objects (3.8 by 4.7 degrees of visual angle) under inattention, divided attention, and full attention conditions, with scenes presented for 100 ms followed by a pattern mask. In the inattention condition, 60 per cent of participants reported only the cross, and those who noticed the scenes often normalized incongruent objects, such as mistaking a girl licking a light bulb for eating ice cream. With divided attention, 70 per cent noticed scenes but normalized incongruities, while in the full attention condition, 90 per cent noticed scenes but did not identify incongruities, normalizing them instead. Increasing the scene size to 5.7 by 7.05 degrees did not significantly improve detection of incongruities, as 40 per cent in the inattention condition, 90 per cent in the divided attention condition, and 80 per cent in the full attention condition still normalized incongruent objects. Extending the presentation time to 200 ms also did not improve detection; 50 per cent in the inattention, 70 per cent in the divided attention, and 90 per cent in the full attention condition noticed scenes but normalized incongruities. Subsequent experiments involving classifying scenes as 'weird' or 'not weird' and using the flicker paradigm showed that participants often failed to detect incongruities, instead normalizing them. Finally, testing interference of incongruent elements in visual arrays showed no significant perceptual sensitivity differences, with only one participant noticing anything unusual.

These findings indicate that scene incongruity does not reliably capture attention for conscious perception, as participants frequently normalized incongruent objects based on scene gist, even with full attention. Increasing scene size and presentation time did not significantly improve detection of incongruities. In contrast, Clarke and Porubanova (2020) found that scenes with semantic violations are perceived as lasting longer, indicating that unexpected features in scenes require more cognitive processing time, leading to subjective time dilation. Their study, which involved larger stimuli presented for longer durations, revealed that processing incongruities increases perceived time. Tachmatzidou and Vatakis (2023) further explored the impact of semantic and syntactic violations on time perception, showing that semantic violations led to time compression, while syntactic violations led to time dilation. They also found that increasing the contrast of target objects amplified these effects, highlighting the role of attention in modulating duration perception. The differing results between Clarke and Porubanova (2020) and Tachmatzidou and Vatakis (2023) regarding semantic violations may stem from methodological differences. Moreover, the discrepancy between

Mack et al. (2017) and Clarke and Porubanova (2020) could be attributed to the size and duration of the stimuli used, suggesting that these factors play a crucial role in the perception of incongruent scenes. Further investigation is needed to understand the underlying mechanisms of how different types of violations and various stimulus characteristics affect attention and perception, and to clarify the roles of scene size, duration, and contrast in these processes. This could involve systematically varying these parameters to discern their individual and combined effects on the conscious perception of scene incongruities.

6.4 Evidence from Cognitive Neuroscience

Jiang et al. (2013) investigated the interaction between attention and expectation in visual perception using fMRI. Participants engaged in tasks with manipulated expectations and attention, where they viewed faces and scenes paired with predictive auditory cues. They found that attention enhances the precision of prediction errors, making expected and unexpected stimuli more distinct at the neural level. The results indicated that attention and expectation enhance category selectivity through different neural mechanisms, with attention affecting higher cortical levels and expectation modulating lower cortical levels.

Gordon et al. (2019) used EEG and hierarchical frequency tagging (HFT) to explore how attention and expectation modulate the integration of top-down and bottom-up signals in visual perception. They revealed that attention and expectation influence signal integration through different neural pathways, with expectation affecting descending signals and attention modulating ascending signals. This study provides physiological evidence that attention and expectation optimize perceptual processing via distinct mechanisms.

Expectation, in this context, primarily influences descending signals, meaning it shapes the predictive frameworks the brain uses to process incoming sensory information. This top-down modulation is consistent with the idea that the brain constantly generates and updates models to predict sensory input, thereby facilitating perceptual processing when the actual input aligns with these predictions (Clark, 2013; Hohwy, 2013).

On the other hand, attention modulates ascending signals, meaning it enhances the processing of incoming sensory information by prioritizing relevant stimuli. This modulation aligns with extensive neuroscientific evidence showing that attention can amplify neural responses to attended stimuli, thereby enhancing their salience in the perceptual processing stream (Kastner & Ungerleider, 2000; Martinez et al., 2007; Mehrpour et al., 2020).

Duyar et al. (2024) explored the interaction between temporal attention and expectation in visual perception. Their study demonstrated that voluntary temporal attention and expectation jointly enhance perceptual accuracy and neural responses. Using tasks requiring participants to focus on specific time intervals and predict visual stimuli, they found that attention and expectation synergistically improve the processing of events, revealing their combined importance in optimizing perceptual performance.

The evidence suggests that attention generally enhances sensory inputs through the facilitation of ascending signals, while expectation shapes perception by refining the brain's predictive models, thus affecting descending signals (Clark, 2013; Friston, 2005). However, it is important to note that attention not only facilitates but also inhibits processing. For example, Reynolds and Heeger (2009) found that attention can suppress the processing of irrelevant stimuli, thereby reducing their interference with the attended information. Therefore, it is clear that both mechanisms are integral to attention and expectation. Research indicates that attention involves both facilitatory and inhibitory processes depending on the context and task demands (Carrasco, 2011; Reynolds & Heeger, 2009). This perspective is consistent with the broader body of behavioural and neuroscientific data on the top-down effects of attention, which enhance perceptual sensitivity and cognitive processing efficiency (e.g., Jiang et al., 2013; Carrasco et al., 2004).

7 Expectation Awareness: Seeing What Is Not There

7.1 Expectation Causes Illusory Perception without Attention

Expectations can lead us to see what is not there, even without attention. This section examines the evidence supporting this phenomenon and discusses experimental research showing how expectations may cause illusory perceptions in the absence of stimuli.

Mack et al. (2016) explored the role of attention in IM and its relationship with expectations. This study aimed to determine whether IM can exist without attention. In this experiment, participants were presented with a matrix of letters at fixation and the circle task described earlier. The probability of reporting whether the four circles were the same or whether one was different was 90 per cent, which led the participants to attend more to the circle task than reporting the letters in the matrix. This demanding task allowed the researchers to explore what is perceived without attention. On the critical 101st trial, with their attention maximally diverted from the matrix, participants were instructed to report letters from the matrix, which were, in fact, not presented. More than half of the participants reported seeing a matrix of letters not present on the screen. When asked to enter the letters they 'saw', participants wrote down letters, suggesting an illusory perception.

The researchers explored this in another study (Erol et al., 2016). Participants reported the longer arm of a cross in the visual periphery while a colour-filled circle, alternating between blue and yellow from trial to trial, appeared at fixation on every trial except for the critical trials. On the critical trial, only the cross appeared. Participants were tested under inattention, divided attention, and full attention conditions. In the inattention condition, after twenty-five trials with the cross and coloured circle, only three of the fifteen participants reported the absence of the coloured circle, while the remaining twelve reported seeing either a blue or yellow circle despite its absence. In the divided attention condition, participants reported both the longer arm of the cross and anything else they noticed. Seven of the fifteen participants in the critical trial were unaware of the circle's absence and incorrectly reported seeing it. In the full attention condition, participants were instructed to ignore the cross and report anything else on the screen. Here, fourteen of the fifteen participants correctly identified the absence of the circle on the critical trial. This significant difference in awareness between the inattention and full attention conditions demonstrates a powerful effect of expectation in visual perception: the illusion of seeing a stimulus even when it is not present.

In another study, Erol et al. (2018) explored this phenomenon with a highly meaningful stimulus – a face. In non-critical trials, participants reported whether four colour-bisected circles surrounding a face at fixation were the same or different. On the final critical trial, the face was absent. They found that 73.3 per cent of participants in the inattention condition reported seeing a face when it was absent, 46.7 per cent in the divided attention condition, and 0 per cent in the full attention condition. Conversely, when the face was present, 66.7 per cent of participants in the inattention condition, 93.3 per cent in the divided attention condition, and 100 per cent in the full attention condition reported seeing it. These findings illustrate the significant influence of unintentionally formed expectations on perception, leading to illusory perceptions of faces even when they are not present.

Aru and Bachmann (2017) conducted a study to replicate and extend the findings of Mack et al. (2016). They used the Perceptual Awareness Scale (PAS), which measures the subjective visibility of letters. This scale allowed participants to rate their experience of the letter array from 1 ('no experience of the stimulus') to 4 ('clear impression of the stimulus'). In the dual-task condition, where attention was primarily diverted to the circles (cued 90 per cent of the time), on the 101st trial, no letters were presented, yet participants rated their visibility. The results revealed that six out of seventeen participants did not notice the absence of letters and rated the visibility of the non-existent letters similarly to trials where letters were present. These participants gave an average rating of 2.7 for the non-existent letters, indicating an 'almost clear impression of the stimulus'.

In a later study, Aru et al. (2018) developed dual-task setups to investigate how expectations might lead to illusory perceptions without attention. Across three experiments, participants engaged in a primary task while occasionally being queried about an auxiliary task designed to induce expectations. In the first experiment, participants viewed faces with surrounding squares and rated the visibility of these squares. Despite the squares being absent in critical trials, over 90 per cent of participants reported seeing them at least once, with many giving high visibility ratings. Only one participant never rated the visibility higher than 1 ('no experience of the stimulus') across the six critical trials. On average, participants reported some experience of the missing stimulus in 50 per cent of the critical trials, with six of the fourteen participants perceiving illusory squares on more than three occasions, and nine participants rating the visibility as 'almost clear' at least once. Interestingly, the study found a negative correlation between Autism Spectrum Quotient (AQ) scores and the frequency of these illusory perceptions, suggesting that individuals with higher autistic traits were less susceptible to such illusions.

In the second experiment, participants were asked to discriminate between the orientation of the faces or report the visibility of a small Landolt square, a figure consisting of a square with a gap on one side, and which was absent on critical trials. The findings were consistent with the first experiment, as 67 per cent of critical trials involved reports of experiencing the absent stimulus. Twelve out of fifteen used the rating 'almost clear expression' for the absent stimulus at least once, and six participants reported a 'clear impression' of the missing stimulus. This demonstrated a strong effect of expectations on perception, even in a setup designed to divert attention from the auxiliary task.

The third experiment further supported these findings. Participants had to identify odd-coloured circles or rate the visibility of non-existent letters. Out of the seventeen participants, three did not experience any illusory perception, but six participants had illusory perceptions in more than half of the trials. Seven participants rated the visibility as 'almost clear' at least once, and four reported a 'clear impression' of the missing stimulus on at least one trial.

These experiments consistently showed that participants often reported perceiving stimuli that were not present, with varying degrees of illusory perception influenced by task difficulty and attentional demands. Notably, even under conditions designed to divert attentional focus from the auxiliary task, expectations still led to high rates of illusory perceptions. The results suggest that even when no letters, colour patches, or faces were present, participants' brains 'filled in the gap' with expected content, leading to the perception of a stimulus that was not there. These findings reveal the power of experimentally induced expectations in creating vivid illusory perceptions in the absence of attention: expectation awareness. Both IB and expectation awareness can be explained by the predictive processing framework. This is the topic of the next section.

7.2 Expectation Awareness and Inattentional Blindness: A Simple Predictive Processing Model

Expectation awareness and IB reveal the interwoven dynamics of attention and expectation in shaping perceptual experiences. This section will examine how predictive coding can explain the phenomena of IB and expectation awareness.

7.2.1 Expectation Awareness: Predictive Coding Explanation

Expectation awareness arises within the predictive coding framework when high precision is assigned to predictions and low precision is assigned to sensory inputs. When participants expect a stimulus, the brain generates strong prior predictions (high precision on priors). If attention is focused elsewhere, the precision of sensory input from the expected location is low. Consequently, any prediction errors resulting from the absence of the stimulus are given little weight, and the strong prior prediction dominates perception, leading to an illusory experience (Hohwy, 2012). This can be mathematically illustrated with the following equations:

Prediction Error Calculation •

Prediction Error Calculation:

$$\epsilon = y - \mu$$

Precision-Weighted Prediction Error:

$$\tilde{\epsilon} = \Pi\epsilon$$

Updating Predictions:

$$\Delta\mu = \eta\tilde{\epsilon}$$

Here, y represents sensory input, μ represents the prediction, Π represents precision, and η is the learning rate. $\tilde{\epsilon}$ is precision-weighted prediction error.

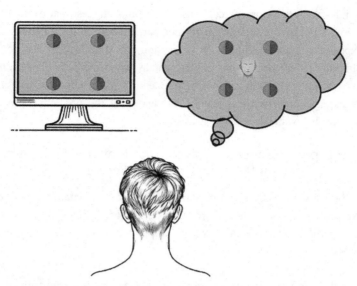

Figure 7 Expectation awareness. This illustrates how inattention and prior
expectations can lead to perceiving stimuli that are not present.

In the case of expectation awareness, Π is low for sensory input and high for
predictions, resulting in a perceptual experience dominated by the prior prediction (see Figure 7).

7.2.2 Inattentional Blindness: Predictive Coding Explanation

Predictive coding explains IB by focusing on the low precision assigned to
unattended sensory inputs. When attention is directed towards a task, the precision
of sensory input related to that task is high, ensuring accurate perception of task-
relevant stimuli. However, the precision of unattended sensory inputs is low, reducing the impact of prediction errors and leading to failures in noticing unexpected
stimuli (Dehaene et al., 2006). This can be expressed mathematically as follows:

When attention is high on the task:

$$\tilde{\epsilon}_{high} = \Pi_{high} \cdot (y - \mu)$$

When attention is low on unexpected stimuli:

$$\tilde{\epsilon}_{low} = \Pi_{low} \cdot (y - \mu)$$

Here, Π is high for task-relevant inputs, resulting in a strong updating of
predictions based on these inputs. Conversely, Π is low for unexpected stimuli,
leading to minimal updating of predictions and IB (see Figure 8).

Figure 8 Inattentional blindness. This illustrates how focused attention on a task can lead to missing unexpected objects.

7.2.3 Unified Model: Attention and Expectation

Combining both phenomena, the unified model describes how perception balances sensory inputs and prior predictions, moderated by the precision assigned to each.

1. When Attention is High (Task-Focused):

   $\tilde{\epsilon}\_task = \Pi\_task(y - \mu)$

   Here, Π_task is high, resulting in strong prediction updates for task-relevant inputs.

2. When Attention is Low (Unattended Stimuli):

   $\tilde{\epsilon}\_unattended = \Pi\_unattended(y - \mu)$

   Here, $\Pi\_unattended$ is low, leading to minimal updates and higher chances of IB.

3. When Expectation is High (Expecting a Stimulus):

   $\tilde{\epsilon}\_high\_expectation = \Pi\_high\_expectation(y - \mu)$

   Here, $\Pi\_high\_expectation$ is high, leading to a perceptual experience dominated by the prediction, even if the sensory input is absent.

4. When Sensory Input is Low Precision (Strong Expectation but Low Sensory Evidence):

$$\tilde{\epsilon}\_low\_sensory = \Pi\_low\_sensory(y - \mu)$$

Here, $\Pi\_low\_sensory$ is low, leading to an illusory experience driven by the prior prediction.

The unified model posits that perceptual experiences are shaped by precision-weighted prediction errors. The precision (Π) determines the influence of either the sensory input or the prediction on perception. High precision on predictions can lead to expectation awareness and illusory perceptions, while high precision on sensory inputs can mitigate IB. Conversely, low precision on unattended sensory inputs increases the likelihood of IB, while low precision on sensory inputs under high-expectation conditions promotes illusory perceptions. This model can be tested through various psychophysical experiments that manipulate the precision of sensory inputs and predictions, providing empirical validation for the theoretical framework.

To illustrate, imagine you are standing on the corner of Regent's Street and Piccadilly. You have left the café and are now waiting for your friend to arrive. The environment is teeming with activity: people walking, cars honking, and shop-fronts displaying vibrant advertisements. However, your primary focus is on spotting your friend as she approaches. Your brain uses past experiences and context to predict the street scene. Based on your memory of this location, you expect to see pedestrians, vehicles, and familiar storefronts. At a more immediate level, your brain predicts the visual details of your friend, such as her appearance and walking pattern. Your attention is sharply focused on the spot where you expect your friend to appear. This high-precision weighting ensures that any sensory input from this region is processed more accurately. The rest of the street scene receives lower precision weighting, meaning your brain allocates fewer attentional resources to these areas.

As you scan the crowd, sensory inputs (visual, auditory, etc.) continuously stream in. When your friend appears, your brain quickly matches the sensory input with the high-precision prediction of her appearance, resulting in low prediction error. In peripheral areas where your attention is not focused, expectations dominate. Although you are not actively attending to the entire street, your brain constructs a coherent scene by filling in gaps with expected elements. You might not perceive every pedestrian or car consciously, but your brain uses past experiences to create a plausible background.

While you are focused on your friend, significant changes in the unattended parts of the scene (e.g., a bus about to drive through a big puddle or a person tripping) might go unnoticed due to IB. Your brain continues to use stored predictions to maintain a consistent perception of the street. Your conscious experience of the busy street is woven from the high-fidelity perception of your friend and the low-fidelity, expectation-driven fill-ins for the rest of the scene. This creates a seamless and coherent experience, even though parts of it are constructed from predictions rather than directly based on sensory input. As you shift your focus or if something unexpected happens (e.g., a loud noise), your brain rapidly updates its predictions and reallocates attentional resources to minimize prediction errors and adjust your conscious experience accordingly.

This view of attention as precision finds support from Hohwy (2012), who explained IB similarly. He writes:

> If the gain on one signal is turned up, then the gain on the other signals must be turned down. Otherwise the notion of gain is meaningless: weights must sum to one. So, as expectations for precision turn up the gain on one prediction error, the gain for others will be turned down. In addition, it may be that the cues increase the prior probability of a validly cued target, as we saw in the discussion of the Posner paradigm. If a weaker, low-precision stimulus is shown in the non-cued region, it will struggle against both low gain and low prior probability. As a result, this stimulus may never be perceived . . . This very nicely maps on to the phenomenon known as inattentional blindness. (Hohwy, 2012, p. 199)

We can explain expectation awareness under the same elegant framework. When high precision is assigned to an expected prediction, the gain on this prediction is increased, leading to a decrease in the gain on other predictions. As a result, when the brain assigns high precision to an expected stimulus, the gain for other sensory inputs, particularly those that do not align with the expectation, is reduced. In this scenario, cues that increase the prior probability of the expected stimulus further enhance its precision. This means that the brain's strong prediction about the presence of a particular stimulus becomes dominant. If a stimulus that contradicts this expectation is presented, it receives low precision and is less likely to influence perception. The prediction error from this unexpected stimulus is down-weighted, and the strong prior expectation continues to shape the perceptual experience.

Therefore, expectation awareness occurs when the brain's high-precision predictions dominate perception, even without corresponding sensory input. The brain effectively 'fills in' the expected stimulus based on strong prior predictions, leading to an illusory experience. This phenomenon illustrates how perceptual systems rely on expectations, particularly when attention is diverted elsewhere, resulting in the illusory perception of stimuli that are not present.

Predictive processing provides a robust framework for integrating the roles of attention and expectation in shaping perceptual experiences. Attention enhances the precision of sensory inputs and prediction errors, ensuring that attended stimuli have a greater impact on updating predictions. When attention is focused on a task, the precision of sensory input related to that task is high, leading to more accurate and rapid processing. Conversely, when attention is diverted, the precision of sensory input is low, causing the brain to rely more heavily on prior expectations, resulting in phenomena such as IB and expectation awareness.

This model has implications for understanding how we navigate our environment. It suggests that perception is not a passive reception of sensory data but an active construction process where the brain continually predicts and updates its internal model of the world. Attention and expectation are critical components of this process, dynamically adjusting the precision of sensory inputs and predictions to optimize perception and behaviour. Precision weighting can thus be seen as a mechanism for modulating consciousness—in terms of what becomes a conscious experience and what remains unconscious or backgrounded. Under this view, consciousness is a dynamic process driven by the brain's need to manage precision-weighted prediction errors—helping the brain balance internal expectations with external reality.

8 Implications and Future Research

Throughout this Element, we have explored the dynamics of attention and expectation and their influence on visual experience. Our journey began with the question: is attention necessary for conscious perception, or can conscious experiences occur without it? While the evidence reviewed strongly suggests that without attention, we do not consciously *perceive* the world, 'expectation awareness' tantalizingly suggests that not all visual experiences (e.g., hallucinations) require attention.

These findings pose a challenge to the Global Workspace Theory (GWT) and other scientific theories of consciousness (Kuhn, 2024), such as the Attention Schema Theory (AST), which posit attention as necessary for consciousness (Graziano, 2013; Mashour et al., 2020). GWT, proposed by Baars (Baars, 1997) and further developed by Dehaene et al. (Dehaene & Naccache, 2001; Dehaene et al., 1998), suggests that consciousness arises from the integration and broadcasting of information across specialized brain processors. This theory posits that information becomes conscious when it is broadcasted within a global neuronal workspace (GNW), allowing it to be accessed by various cognitive processes. Attention is considered a critical mechanism for selecting and amplifying information for this global broadcasting, making it a prerequisite for conscious experience. According to AST, the brain constructs a simplified model of its own attention processes, called the 'attention schema'. This model helps the brain monitor and control attention, and it is this internal representation that is consciousness. According to AST, attention is fundamental for consciousness, as the brain's model of its attentional state is what creates conscious experience.

The evidence that illusory perceptions can arise from strong expectations without the need for attentional mechanisms (expectation awareness) indicates that consciousness can occur without direct attentional engagement, questioning the necessity of attention for conscious processing as proposed by GWT and AST. This suggests that other cognitive processes, particularly those involving predictive mechanisms, play a significant role in generating conscious experience. Given this, integrating these theories with predictive coding may provide a more explanatory and predictive framework for understanding consciousness. This would be a good research programme to pursue.

These findings also have clinical implications. Expectation awareness has similarities with phenomena typically described as hallucinations (Bachmann, 2021). Both involve illusory perceptions without corresponding external stimuli. This suggests a nuanced understanding of hallucinations – they are not merely symptoms of pathology or drug effects but can also be manifestations of the brain's normal operation under extreme predictive biases (Corlett et al., 2019; K. J. Friston, 2005; Powers et al., 2016; Powers et al., 2017; Suzuki et al., 2017). Friston posits that hallucinations result from the brain's misestimation of the precision of sensory inputs and priors. When the brain's cholinergic mechanisms, which balance bottom-up sensory evidence and top-down priors, are dysfunctional, this balance is disrupted, leading to hallucinations. This model aligns with observations in schizophrenia, where hallucinations are prevalent and often associated with impaired cholinergic function (Fletcher & Frith, 2007; K. J. Friston, 2005).

Perception has been described as a controlled hallucination: perceptual experiences are actively constructed by the brain's top-down predictions, which are calibrated by bottom-up sensory inputs. In normal perception, this interaction keeps experiences aligned with external reality. During hallucinations, however, these sensory signals fail to properly constrain the brain's predictions, resulting in perceptions that are not tied to actual external stimuli. Thus, normal perception and hallucination may exist on a continuum, with hallucination being an extreme form of perception driven by unchecked predictive processes (Seth, 2021; Clark, 2013; see Suzuki et al.'s Hallucination Machine experiments, in which, using a combination of VR and deep convolutional neural networks, participants experienced phenomenology similar to that experienced with psychedelics).

Future research should further explore expectation awareness and the interaction between attention and expectation in conscious perception. One important avenue of research involves measuring the neural correlates of expectation awareness, as we are currently doing in my lab. In a recent study (Tyler & Clarke, in preparation), we replicated the earlier findings of Erol et al. (2018), who found that a strong expectation of seeing a face led to an illusory perception of a face, and showed this effect was correlated with participants' visual imagery abilities, as measured by their visual imagery scores. We are currently planning an ERP experiment to explore this further. A known ERP associated with face perception is the N170, a negative waveform occurring in the occipitotemporal cortex around 170 ms after the presentation of a face stimulus. We predict that if the participant hallucinates a face in its absence, we should see an N170, weaker than when the face is present but stronger than when it is absent. This would suggest that the participant is having an experience of the face, driven by their strong prior expectations. This study could provide significant insights into the neural mechanisms underlying expectation awareness and further validate the predictive coding model.

Future research should also explore expectation awareness with various scenes, animations, patterns, and objects to see how powerful this effect can be. Do observers hallucinate the gist of a scene under conditions of inattention and high expectation that the scene will be present? Do they hallucinate gardens, cityscapes, or mountains? Such studies would expand our understanding of the extent and limitations of expectation-driven perception and further elucidate the mechanisms behind conscious experience.

9 Concluding Remarks

In conclusion, while the evidence strongly suggests that without some form of attention, we do not consciously *perceive* the visual world, its scenes, objects, and object properties (Mack & Rock, 1998), several research labs have found evidence that under conditions of inattention, when we are not attending to the spatial location of an object but expecting it to be there, we may hallucinate a stimulus in its absence. This suggests that expectation alone can generate a conscious experience independent of attention.

The study of attention and expectation through the predictive processing framework offers a comprehensive understanding of perception, demonstrating the effect of both in constructing an internal model of the world. The constructive nature of visual experience is beautifully captured in an observation by Leonardo da Vinci. In the following, he advises painters on techniques to inspire artistic creation. He writes:

> You should look at certain walls stained with damp, or at stones of uneven colour. If you have to invent some backgrounds, you will be able to see in these the likeness of divine landscapes, adorned with mountains, ruins, rocks, woods, great plains, hills and valleys in great variety; and then again, you will see there battles and strange figures in violent action. . . . In such walls, the same thing happens as in the sound of bells, in whose stroke you may find every named word you can imagine. (quoted from Gombrich (2023, p. 159))

Here the artist evocatively captures the power of the predictive mind. Just as one can mentally build imagined scenes, figures, and actions from the ambiguous patterns on the stained wall, current evidence and theory from the cognitive sciences suggest brains construct perceptual reality based on mechanisms of attention and expectation to infer the world from the ever-changing ambiguous patterns impinging on the sensory receptors.

References

Adams, W. J., Graf, E. W., & Ernst, M. O. (2004). Experience can change the 'light-from-above' prior. *Nature Neuroscience, 7*(10), 1057–1058. https://doi.org/10.1038/nn1312.

Aitchison, L., & Lengyel, M. (2017). With or without you: Predictive coding and Bayesian inference in the brain. *Current Opinion in Neurobiology, 46*, 219–227. https://doi.org/10.1016/j.conb.2017.08.010.

Alink, A., Schwiedrzik, C. M., Kohler, A., Singer, W., & Muckli, L. (2010). Stimulus predictability reduces responses in primary visual cortex. *The Journal of Neuroscience, 30*(8), 2960–2966. https://doi.org/10.1523/JNEUROSCI.3730-10.2010.

Amir, Y. Z., Assaf, Y., Yovel, Y., & Mudrik, L. (2023). Experiencing without knowing? Empirical evidence for phenomenal consciousness without access. *Cognition, 238*, 105529. https://doi.org/10.1016/j.cognition.2023.105529.

Aru, J., Bachmann, T., Singer, W., & Melloni, L. (2012). Distilling the neural correlates of consciousness. *Neuroscience and Biobehavioral Reviews, 36*(2), 737–746. https://doi.org/10.1016/j.neubiorev.2011.12.003.

Aru, J., & Bachmann, T. (2017). Expectation creates something out of nothing: The role of attention in iconic memory reconsidered. *Consciousness and Cognition, 53*, 203–210. https://doi.org/10.1016/j.concog.2017.06.017.

Aru, J., Tulver, K., & Bachmann, T. (2018). It's all in your head: Expectations create illusory perception in a dual-task setup. *Consciousness and Cognition, 65*, 197–208. https://doi.org/10.1016/j.concog.2018.09.001.

Aru, J., Suzuki, M., Rutiku, R., Larkum, M. E., & Bachmann, T. (2019). Coupling the state and contents of consciousness. *Frontiers in Systems Neuroscience, 13*, 43.

Averbach, E., & Coriell, A. S. (1961). Short-term memory in vision. *Bell System Technical Journal, 40*, 309–328. https://doi.org/10.1002/j.1538-7305.1961.tb03987.x.

Baars, B. J. (1993). *A cognitive theory of consciousness.* Cambridge, UK: Cambridge University Press.

Baars, B. J. (1997). In the theatre of consciousness: Global workspace theory, a rigorous scientific theory of consciousness. *Journal of Consciousness Studies, 4*(4), 292–309.

Bachmann, T., Breitmeyer, B. G., & Öğmen, H. (2011). *The experimental phenomena of consciousness: A brief dictionary revised edition.* New York: Oxford University Press.

Bachmann, T. (2021). 'Normal' hallucinations and attention. *Frontiers in Neuroscience, 15*, 731600. https://doi.org/10.3389/fnins.2021.731600.

Bachmann, T., & Aru, J. (2023). Conscious interpretation: A distinct aspect for the neural markers of the contents of consciousness. *Consciousness and Cognition, 108*, 103471. https://doi.org/10.1016/j.concog.2023.103471.

Bar, M. (2004). Visual objects in context. *Nature Reviews Neuroscience, 5*(8), 617–629. https://doi.org/10.1038/nrn1476.

Bar, M., & Ullman, S. (1996). Spatial context in recognition. *Perception, 25*(3), 343–352. https://doi.org/10.1068/p250343.

Bayes, T. (1763). An essay towards solving a problem in the doctrine of chances. *Philosophical Transactions of the Royal Society of London, 53*, 370–418. https://doi.org/10.1098/rstl.1763.0053.

Bayne, T., Hohwy, J., & Owen, A. M. (2016). Are there levels of consciousness? *Trends in Cognitive Sciences, 20*(6), 405–413. https://doi.org/10.1016/j.tics .2016.03.009.

Becker, M. W., Pashler, H., & Anstis, S. M. (2000). The role of iconic memory in change-detection tasks. *Perception, 29*(3), 273–286. https://doi.org/ 10.1068/p3035.

Berkeley, G. (1948). An essay toward a new theory of vision, 1709. In W. Dennis (Ed.), *Readings in the history of psychology* (pp. 69–80). New York: Appleton-Century-Crofts. https://doi.org/10.1037/11304-009.

Biederman, I., Glass, A. L., & Stacy, E. W. (1973). Searching for objects in real-world scenes. *Journal of Experimental Psychology, 97*(1), 22–27. https:// doi.org/10.1037/h0033776.

Biederman, I., Rabinowitz, J. C., Glass, A. L., & Stacy, E. W. (1974). On the information extracted from a glance at a scene. *Journal of Experimental Psychology, 103*(3), 597–600. https://doi.org/10.1037/h0037158.

Biederman, I. (1981). On the semantics of a glance at a scene. In M. Kubovy, & J. R. Pomerantz (Eds.), *Perceptual Organization* (pp. 213–253). Hillsdale, NJ: Erlbaum.

Biederman, I., Mezzanotte, R. J., & Rabinowitz, J. C. (1982). Scene perception: Detecting and judging objects undergoing relational violations. *Cognitive Psychology, 14*(2), 143–177. https://doi.org/10.1016/0010-0285(82)90007-x.

Bisley, J. W., & Goldberg, M. E. (2010). Attention, intention, and priority in the parietal lobe. *Annual Review of Neuroscience, 33*, 1–21. https://doi.org/ 10.1146/annurev-neuro-060909-152823.

Blackmore, S. (2005). *Consciousness: A very short introduction.* Oxford: Oxford University Press. https://doi.org/10.1093/actrade/9780192805850 .001.0001.

Blackmore, S. J., Brelstaff, G., Nelson, K., & Trościanko, T. (1995). Is the richness of our visual world an illusion? Transsaccadic memory for complex scenes. *Perception*, *24*(9), 1075–1081. https://doi.org/10.1068/p241075.

Blake, R., & Logothetis, N. (2002). Visual competition. *Nature Reviews: Neuroscience*, *3*(1), 13–21. https://doi.org/10.1038/nrn701.

Block, N. (1995). On a confusion about a function of consciousness. *Behavioral and Brain Sciences*, *18*(2), 227–287. https://doi.org/10.1017/S0140525X0 0038188.

Block, N. (2005). Two neural correlates of consciousness. *Trends in Cognitive Sciences*, *9*(2), 46–52. https://doi.org/10.1016/j.tics.2004.12.006.

Block, N. (2007). Consciousness, accessibility, and the mesh between psychology and neuroscience. *Behavioral and Brain Sciences*, *30*(5–6), 481–499. https://doi:10.1017/S0140525X07002786.

Block, N. (2011). Perceptual consciousness overflows cognitive access. *Trends in cognitive sciences*, *15*(12), 567–575. https://doi.org/10.1016/j.tics.2011.11.001.

Bola, M., & Doradzińska, Ł. (2021). Perceptual awareness negativity – does it reflect awareness or attention? *Frontiers in Human Neuroscience*, *15*, 742513.

Bonneh, Y., Cooperman, A., & Sagi, D. (2001). Motion-induced blindness in normal observers. *Nature*, *411*, 798–801. https://doi.org/10.1038/35081073.

Brandman, T., & Peelen, M. V. (2017). Interaction between scene and object processing revealed by human fMRI and MEG decoding. *The Journal of Neuroscience*, *37*(32), 7700–7710. https://doi.org/10.1523/JNEUROSCI .0582-17.2017.

Breitmeyer, B. G. (2007). Visual masking: Past accomplishments, present status, future developments. *Advances in Cognitive Psychology*, *3*(1–2), 9.

Breitmeyer, B. G., & Öğmen, H. (2006). *Visual masking: Time slices through conscious and unconscious vision* (2nd ed.). Oxford: Oxford University Press. https://doi.org/10.1093/acprof:oso/9780198530671.001.0001.

Breitmeyer, B. G. (2014). *The visual (un)conscious and its (dis)contents: A microtemporal approach*. Oxford: Oxford University Press.

Broadbent, D. E. (1958). *Perception and communication*. Oxford: Pergamon Press.

Bronfman, Z. Z., Brezis, N., Jacobson, H., & Usher, M. (2014). We see more than we can report: 'Cost free' color phenomenality outside focal attention. *Psychological Science*, *25*(7), 1394–1403. https://doi.org/10.1177/095679 7614532656.

Bugelski, B. R., & Alampay, D. A. (1961). The role of frequency in developing perceptual sets. *Canadian Journal of Psychology / Revue canadienne de psychologie*, *15*(4), 205–211. https://doi.org/10.1037/h0083443.

Buschman, T. J., & Miller, E. K. (2007). Top-down versus bottom-up control of attention in the prefrontal and posterior parietal cortices. *Science, 315*(5820), 1860–1862. https://doi.org/10.1126/science.1138071.

Carrasco, M., Penpeci-Talgar, C., & Eckstein, M. (2000). Spatial covert attention increases contrast sensitivity across the CSF: Support for signal enhancement. *Vision Research, 40*(10–12), 1203–1215. https://doi.org/10.1016/s0042-6989(00)00024-9.

Carrasco, M., & McElree, B. (2001). Covert attention accelerates the rate of visual information processing. *Proceedings of the National Academy of Sciences of the United States of America, 98*(9), 5363–5367. https://doi.org/10.1073/pnas.081074098.

Carrasco, M., Williams, P. E., & Yeshurun, Y. (2002). Covert attention increases spatial resolution with or without masks: Support for signal enhancement. *Journal of Vision, 2*(6), 467–479. https://doi.org/10.1167/2.6.4.

Carrasco, M., Ling, S., & Read, S. (2004). Attention alters appearance. *Nature Neuroscience, 7*(3), 308–313. https://doi.org/10.1038/nn1194.

Chun, M. M., & Potter, M. C. (1995). A two-stage model for multiple target detection in rapid serial visual presentation. *Journal of Experimental Psychology: Human Perception and Performance, 21*(1), 109–127. https://doi.org/10.1037//0096-1523.21.1.109.

Ciupińska, K., Orłowska, W., Zębrowski, A., et al. (2024). The influence of spatial and temporal attention on visual awareness-a behavioral and ERP study. *Cerebral Cortex, 34*(6), bhae241. https://doi.org/10.1093/cercor/bhae241.

Clark, A. (2013). Whatever next? Predictive brains, situated agents, and the future of cognitive science. *The Behavioral and Brain Sciences, 36*(3), 181–204. https://doi.org/10.1017/S0140525X12000477.

Clark, A. (2015). *Surfing uncertainty: Prediction, action, and the embodied mind*. Oxford: Oxford University Press.

Clarke, J., & Mack, A. (2015). Iconic memory for natural scenes: Evidence using a modified change-detection procedure. *Visual Cognition, 23*(7), 917–938. https://doi.org/10.1080/13506285.2015.1103826.

Clarke, J., & Porubanova, M. (2020). Scene and object violations cause subjective time dilation. *Timing & Time Perception, 8*(3–4), 279–298. https://doi.org/10.1163/22134468-bja10012.

Cohen, M. A., Alvarez, G. A., & Nakayama, K. (2011). Natural-scene perception requires attention. *Psychological Science, 22*(9), 1165–1172.

Cohen, M. A., & Dennett, D. C. (2011). Consciousness cannot be separated from function. *Trends in Cognitive Sciences, 15*(8), 358–364. https://doi.org/10.1016/j.tics.2011.06.008.

Cohen, M. A., Dennett, D. C., & Kanwisher, N. G. (2016). What is the bandwidth of perceptual experience? *Trends in Cognitive Sciences, 20*, 324–335.

Cohen, M. A., Ortego, K., Kyroudis, A., & Pitts, M. (2020). Distinguishing the neural correlates of perceptual awareness and postperceptual processing. *Journal of Neuroscience, 40*(25), 4925–4935.

Coltheart, M. (1980). Iconic memory and visible persistence. *Perception & Psychophysics, 27*, 183–228.

Coltheart, M., & Coltheart, V. (2010). Visual memories. In V. Coltheart (Ed.), *Tutorials in visual cognition* New York: Psychology Press, Taylor and Francis.

Corbetta, M., & Shulman, G. L. (2002). Control of goal-directed and stimulus-driven attention in the brain. *Nature Reviews Neuroscience, 3*(3), 201–215. https://doi.org/10.1038/nrn755.

Corlett, P. R., Horga, G., Fletcher, P. C., et al. (2019). Hallucinations and strong priors. *Trends in Cognitive Sciences, 23*(2), 114–127.

Cowan, N. (2001). The magical number 4 in short-term memory: A reconsideration of mental storage capacity. *The Behavioral and Brain Sciences, 24*(1), 87–185. https://doi.org/10.1017/s0140525x01003922.

Cowan, N. (2010). The magical mystery four: How is working memory capacity limited, and why? *Current Directions in Psychological Science, 19*(1), 51–57. https://doi.org/10.1177/0963721409359277.

Cowan, N. (2010). Multiple concurrent thoughts: The meaning and developmental neuropsychology of working memory. *Developmental Neuropsychology, 35*(5), 447–474. https://doi.org/10.1080/87565641.2010.494985.

Cowey, A., & Stoerig, P. (2004). Stimulus cueing in blindsight. *Progress in Brain Research, 144*, 261–277. https://doi.org/10.1016/S0079-6123(03)14418-4.

Davenport, J. L., & Potter, M. C. (2004). Scene consistency in object and background perception. *Psychological Science, 15*(8), 559–564. https://doi.org/10.1111/j.0956-7976.2004.00719.x.

Dehaene, S., Kerszberg, M., & Changeux, J. P. (1998). A neuronal model of a global workspace in effortful cognitive tasks. *Proceedings of the National Academy of Sciences, 95*(24), 14529–14534.

Dehaene, S., & Naccache, L. (2001). Towards a cognitive neuroscience of consciousness: Basic evidence and a workspace framework. *Cognition, 79*(1–2), 1–37.

Dehaene, S., Changeux, J. P., Naccache, L., Sackur, J., & Sergent, C. (2006). Conscious, preconscious, and subliminal processing: A testable taxonomy. *Trends in Cognitive Sciences, 10*(5), 204–211. https://doi.org/10.1016/j.tics.2006.03.007.

Dehaene, S., & Changeux, J. P. (2011). Experimental and theoretical approaches to conscious processing. *Neuron, 70*(2), 200–227. https://doi.org/10.1016/j .neuron.2011.03.018.

Dehaene, S., Changeux, J. P., & Naccache, L. (2011). The global neuronal workspace model of conscious access: From neuronal architectures to clinical applications. In S. Dehaene & Y. Christen (Eds.), *Characterizing consciousness: From cognition to the clinic?* (pp. 55–84).

Dembski, C., Koch, C., & Pitts, M. (2021). Perceptual awareness negativity: A physiological correlate of sensory consciousness. *Trends in Cognitive Sciences, 25*(8), 660–670. https://doi.org/10.1016/j.tics.2021.05.009.

Desimone, R., & Duncan, J. (1995). Neural mechanisms of selective visual attention. *Annual Review of Neuroscience, 18*, 193–222. https://doi.org/ 10.1146/annurev.ne.18.030195.001205.

Ding, Y., Hults, C. M., Raja, R., & Simons, D. J. (2023). Similarity of an unexpected object to the attended and ignored objects affects noticing in a sustained inattentional blindness task. *Attention, Perception & Psychophysics, 85*(7), 2150–2169. https://doi.org/10.3758/s13414-023-02794-2.

Doradzińska, Ł. , & Bola, M. (2024). Early electrophysiological correlates of perceptual consciousness are affected by both exogenous and endogenous attention. *Journal of Cognitive Neuroscience, 36*(7), 1297–1324. https://doi .org/10.1162/jocn_a_02156.

Drew, T., Võ, M. L. H., & Wolfe, J. M. (2013). The invisible gorilla strikes again: Sustained inattentional blindness in expert observers. *Psychological Science, 24*(9), 1848–1853.

Duyar, A., Ren, S., & Carrasco, M. (2024). When temporal attention interacts with expectation. *Scientific Reports, 14*(1), 4624. https://doi.org/10.1038/ s41598-024-55399-6.

Egly, R., Driver, J., & Rafal, R. D. (1994). Shifting visual attention between objects and locations: Evidence from normal and parietal lesion subjects. *Journal of Experimental Psychology: General, 123*(2), 161–177. https://doi .org/10.1037/0096-3445.123.2.161.

Egner, T., Monti, J. M., & Summerfield, C. (2010). Expectation and surprise determine neural population responses in the ventral visual stream. *The Journal of Neuroscience, 30*(49), 16601–16608. https://doi.org/10.1523/ JNEUROSCI.2770-10.2010.

Eklund, R., & Wiens, S. (2018). Visual awareness negativity is an early neural correlate of awareness: A preregistered study with two Gabor sizes. *Cognitive, Affective & Behavioral Neuroscience, 18*(1), 176–188. https://doi.org/10.3758/ s13415-018-0562-z.

Eriksen, C. W., & St James, J. D. (1986). Visual attention within and around the field of focal attention: A zoom lens model. *Perception & Psychophysics, 40* (4), 225–240. https://doi.org/10.3758/bf03211502.

Erol, M., Mack, A., Clarke, J., & Bert, J. (2016). Inattentional blindness to absent stimuli: The role of expectation. *Journal of Vision, 16*(12), 40. https://doi.org/10.1167/16.12.40.

Erol, M., Mack, A., & Clarke, J. (2018). Expectation blindness: Seeing a face when there is none. *Journal of Vision, 18*(10), 1115. https://doi.org/10.1167/18.10.1115.

Feldman, H., & Friston, K. J. (2010). Attention, uncertainty, and free-energy. *Frontiers in Human Neuroscience, 4*, 215. https://doi.org/10.3389/fnhum.2010.00215.

Fletcher, P. C., & Frith, C. D. (2009). Perceiving is believing: A Bayesian approach to explaining the positive symptoms of schizophrenia. *Nature Reviews Neuroscience, 10*(1), 48–58.

Förster, J., Koivisto, M., & Revonsuo, A. (2020). ERP and MEG correlates of visual consciousness: The second decade. *Consciousness and Cognition, 80*, 102917.

Frässle, S., Sommer, J., Jansen, A., Naber, M., & Einhäuser, W. (2014). Binocular rivalry: Frontal activity relates to introspection and action but not to perception. *The Journal of Neuroscience, 34*(5), 1738–1747. https://doi.org/10.1523/JNEUROSCI.4403-13.2014.

Friston, K. (2003). Learning and inference in the brain. *Neural Networks, 16*(9), 1325–1352. https://doi.org/10.1016/j.neunet.2003.06.005.

Friston, K. (2005). A theory of cortical responses. *Philosophical Transactions of the Royal Society of London: Series B, Biological Sciences, 360*(1456), 815–836. https://doi.org/10.1098/rstb.2005.1622.

Friston, K. (2010). The free-energy principle: A unified brain theory? *Nature reviews: Neuroscience, 11*(2), 127–138. https://doi.org/10.1038/nrn2787.

Friston, K., Adams, R. A., Perrinet, L., & Breakspear, M. (2012). Perceptions as hypotheses: Saccades as experiments. *Frontiers in Psychology, 3*, 151. https://doi.org/10.3389/fpsyg.2012.00151.

Friston, K. J. (2005). Hallucinations and perceptual inference. *Behavioral and Brain Sciences, 28*(6), 764–766.

Frith, C. D. (2007). The social brain? *Philosophical Transactions of the Royal Society of London: Series B, Biological Sciences, 362*(1480), 671–678. https://doi.org/10.1098/rstb.2006.2003.

Girshick, A. R., Landy, M. S., & Simoncelli, E. P. (2011). Cardinal rules: Visual orientation perception reflects knowledge of environmental statistics. *Nature Neuroscience, 14*(7), 926–932. https://doi.org/10.1038/nn.2831.

Goldreich, D., & Peterson, M. A. (2012). A Bayesian observer replicates convexity context effects in figure-ground perception. *Seeing and Perceiving, 25* (3–4), 365–395. https://doi.org/10.1163/187847612X634445.

Gombrich, E. H. (2023). *Art and illusion: A study in the psychology of pictorial representation.* New York: Phaidon Press.

Gordon, N., Tsuchiya, N., Koenig-Robert, R., & Hohwy, J. (2019). Expectation and attention increase the integration of top-down and bottom-up signals in perception through different pathways. *PLoS Biology, 17*(4), e3000233. https://doi.org/10.1371/journal.pbio.3000233.

Graziano, M. S. A. (2013). *Consciousness and the social brain.* Oxford: Oxford University Press.

Gregory, R. L. (1980). Perceptions as hypotheses. *Philosophical Transactions of the Royal Society of London: Series B, Biological Sciences, 290*(1038), 181–197. https://doi.org/10.1098/rstb.1980.0090.

Grill-Spector, K., & Malach, R. (2004). The human visual cortex. *Annual Review Neuroscience, 27*(1), 649–677.

Harris, A. M., Dux, P. E., & Mattingley, J. B. (2020). Awareness is related to reduced post-stimulus alpha power: A no-report inattentional blindness study. *The European Journal of Neuroscience, 52*(11), 4411–4422. https://doi.org/10.1111/ejn.13947.

Hassabis, D., Kumaran, D., Summerfield, C., & Botvinick, M. (2017). Neuroscience-inspired artificial intelligence. *Neuron, 95*(2), 245–258. https://doi.org/10.1016/j.neuron.2017.06.011.

Haun, A. M., Tononi, G., Koch, C., & Tsuchiya, N. (2017). Are we underestimating the richness of visual experience? *Neuroscience of Consciousness, 2017*(1), niw023. https://doi.org/10.1093/nc/niw023.

He, S., Cavanagh, P., & Intriligator, J. (1996). Attentional resolution and the locus of visual awareness. *Nature, 383*(6598), 334–337. https://doi.org/10.1038/383334a0.

Helmholtz, H. von (1867/1925). *Treatise on physiological optics* (from 3rd German edition, Trans.). Cambridge, MA. Harvard University Press. https://doi.org/10.1037/13536-000.

Hohwy, J. (2009). The neural correlates of consciousness: New experimental approaches needed? *Consciousness and Cognition, 18*(2), 428–438. https://doi.org/10.1016/j.concog.2009.02.006.

Hohwy, J. (2012). Attention and conscious perception in the hypothesis testing brain. *Frontiers in Psychology, 3*, 96. https://doi.org/10.3389/fpsyg.2012.00096.

Hohwy, J. (2013). *The predictive mind.* Oxford: Oxford University Press.

Hohwy, J. (2020). New directions in predictive processing. *Mind & Language, 35*(2), 209–223. https://doi.org/10.1111/mila.12281.

Hollingworth, A., & Henderson, J. M. (1999). Object identification is isolated from scene semantic constraint: Evidence from object type and token discrimination. *Acta Psychologica, 102*(2–3), 319–343. https://doi.org/10.1016/s0001-6918(98)00053-5.

Hsieh, P. J., Colas, J. T., & Kanwisher, N. (2011). Pop-out without awareness: Unseen feature singletons capture attention only when top-down attention is available. *Psychological Science, 22*(9), 1220–1226. https://doi.org/10.1177/0956797611419302.

Hubel, D. H., & Wiesel, T. N. (1959). Receptive fields of single neurones in the cat's striate cortex. *The Journal of Physiology, 148*(3), 574–591. https://doi.org/10.1113/jphysiol.1959.sp006308.

Hubel, D. H., & Wiesel, T. N. (1962). Receptive fields, binocular interaction and functional architecture in the cat's visual cortex. *The Journal of Physiology, 160*(1), 106–154. https://doi.org/10.1113/jphysiol.1962.sp006837.

Jackson-Nielsen, M., Cohen, M. A., & Pitts, M. A. (2017). Perception of ensemble statistics requires attention. *Consciousness and Cognition, 48*, 149–160. https://doi.org/10.1016/j.concog.2016.11.007.

James, W. (1890). *The principles of psychology.* New York: Dover.

Jeffreys, H. (1998). *Theory of probability.* Oxford: Oxford University Press. https://doi.org/10.1002/wcs.130.

Jensen, M. S., Yao, R., Street, W. N., & Simons, D. J. (2011). Change blindness and inattentional blindness: Wiley interdisciplinary reviews. *Cognitive Science, 2*(5), 529–546. https://doi.org/10.1002/wcs.130.

Jiang, Y., Costello, P., & He, S. (2007). Processing of invisible stimuli: Advantage of upright faces and recognizable words in overcoming interocular suppression. *Psychological Science, 18*(4), 349–355. https://doi.org/10.1111/j.1467-9280.2007.01902.x.

Jiang, J., Summerfield, C., & Egner, T. (2013). Attention sharpens the distinction between expected and unexpected percepts in the visual brain. *The Journal of Neuroscience, 33*(47), 18438–18447. https://doi.org/10.1523/JNEUROSCI.3308-13.2013.

Jimenez, M., Poch, C., Villalba-García, C., et al. (2021). The level of processing modulates visual awareness: Evidence from behavioral and electrophysiological measures. *Journal of Cognitive Neuroscience, 33*(7), 1295–1310.

Jolicoeur, P., & Dell'Acqua, R. (1998). The demonstration of short-term consolidation. *Cognitive Psychology, 36*(2), 138–202. https://doi.org/10.1006/cogp.1998.0684.

Jones, M., & Wilkinson, S. (2020). From prediction to imagination. In A. Abraham (Ed.), *The Cambridge handbook of the imagination* (pp. 94–110). Cambridge: Cambridge University Press.

Kant, I. (2001). *Prolegomena to any future metaphysics* (J. W. Ellington, Trans.). Indianapolis, IN: Hackett. (Original work published 1783).

Kanwisher, N., McDermott, J., & Chun, M. M. (1997). The fusiform face area: A module in human extrastriate cortex specialized for face perception. *The Journal of Neuroscience, 17*(11), 4302–4311. https://doi.org/10.1523/JNEUROSCI.17-11-04302.1997.

Kastner, S., & Ungerleider, L. G. (2000). Mechanisms of visual attention in the human cortex. *Annual Review of Neuroscience, 23*, 315–341. https://doi.org/10.1146/annurev.neuro.23.1.315.

Kentridge, R. W., Heywood, C. A., & Weiskrantz, L. (1999). Attention without awareness in blindsight. *Proceedings: Biological Sciences, 266*(1430), 1805–1811. https://doi.org/10.1098/rspb.1999.0850.

Kentridge, R. W., Heywood, C. A., & Weiskrantz, L. (2004). Spatial attention speeds discrimination without awareness in blindsight. *Neuropsychologia, 42*(6), 831–835.

Kentridge, R. W., Nijboer, T. C. W., & Heywood, C. A. (2008). Attended but unseen: Visual attention is not sufficient for visual awareness. *Neuropsychologia, 46*(3), 864–869. https://doi.org/10.1016/j.neuropsychologia.2007.11.036.

Kersten, D., Mamassian, P., & Yuille, A. (2004). Object perception as Bayesian inference. *Annual Review of Psychology, 55*, 271–304. https://doi.org/10.1146/annurev.psych.55.090902.142005.

Kim, C. Y., & Blake, R. (2005). Psychophysical magic: Rendering the visible 'invisible'. *Trends in Cognitive Sciences, 9*(8), 381–388. https://doi.org/10.1016/j.tics.2005.06.012.

Kloosterman, N. A., Meindertsma, T., van Loon, A. M., et al. (2015). Pupil size tracks perceptual content and surprise. *European Journal of Neuroscience, 41*(8), 1068–1078. https://doi.org/10.1111/ejn.12859.

Knill, D. C., & Pouget, A. (2004). The Bayesian brain: The role of uncertainty in neural coding and computation. *Trends in Neurosciences, 27*(12), 712–719. https://doi.org/10.1016/j.tins.2004.10.007.

Koch, C. (2004). *The quest for consciousness: A neurobiological approach.* Englewood, CO: Roberts.

Koch, C., & Tsuchiya, N. (2007). Attention and consciousness: Two distinct brain processes. *Trends in Cognitive Sciences, 11*(1), 16–22. https://doi.org/10.1016/j.tics.2006.10.012.

Koch, C., Massimini, M., Boly, M., & Tononi, G. (2016). Neural correlates of consciousness: Progress and problems. *Nature Reviews Neuroscience, 17*(5), 307–321. https://doi.org/10.1038/nrn.2016.22.

Koivisto, M., & Revonsuo, A. (2005). Preconscious and conscious processing of color and form: Evidence from event-related potentials. *Consciousness*

and Cognition, *14*(1), 232–246. https://doi.org/10.1016/j.concog.2004
.08.001.

Koivisto, M., & Revonsuo, A. (2007). Electrophysiological correlates of visual consciousness and selective attention. *Neuroreport*, *18*(8), 753–756. https://
doi.org/10.1097/WNR.0b013e3280c143c8.

Koivisto, M., Lähteenmäki, M., Sørensen, T. A., et al. (2008). The earliest electrophysiological correlate of visual awareness? *Brain and Cognition*, *66*
(1), 91–103. https://doi.org/10.1016/j.bandc.2007.05.010.

Koivisto, M., & Revonsuo, A. (2008). Comparison of event-related potentials in attentional blink and repetition blindness. *Brain Research*, *1189*, 115–126.
https://doi.org/10.1016/j.brainres.2007.10.082.

Koivisto, M., Kainulainen, P., & Revonsuo, A. (2009). The relationship between awareness and attention: Evidence from ERP responses. *Neuropsychologia*, *47*
(13), 2891–2899. https://doi.org/10.1016/j.neuropsychologia.2009.06.016.

Koivisto, M., & Revonsuo, A. (2010). Event-related brain potential correlates of visual awareness. *Neuroscience and Biobehavioral Reviews*, *34*(6), 922–934.
https://doi.org/10.1016/j.neubiorev.2009.12.002.

Koivisto, M., Railo, H., Revonsuo, A., Vanni, S., & Salminen-Vaparanta, N. (2011). Recurrent processing in V1/V2 contributes to categorization of natural scenes. *The Journal of Neuroscience*, *31*(7), 2488–2492. https://doi
.org/10.1523/JNEUROSCI.3074-10.2011.

Kok, P., Jehee, J. F., & de Lange, F. P. (2012). Less is more: Expectation sharpens representations in the primary visual cortex. *Neuron*, *75*(2),
265–270. https://doi.org/10.1016/j.neuron.2012.04.034.

Kok, P., Rahnev, D., Jehee, J. F., Lau, H. C., & de Lange, F. P. (2012). Attention reverses the effect of prediction in silencing sensory signals. *Cerebral Cortex*, *22*(9), 2197–2206. https://doi.org/10.1093/cercor/bhr310.

Kok, P., Brouwer, G. J., van Gerven, M. A., & de Lange, F. P. (2013). Prior expectations bias sensory representations in visual cortex. *The Journal of Neuroscience*, *33*(41), 16275–16284. https://doi.org/10.1523/JNEUROSCI
.0742-13.2013.

Kok, P., Failing, M. F., & de Lange, F. P. (2014). Prior expectations evoke stimulus templates in the primary visual cortex. *Journal of Cognitive Neuroscience*, *26*(7), 1546–1554. https://doi.org/10.1162/jocn_a_00562.

Kok, P., Jehee, J. F., & de Lange, F. P. (2012). Less is more: Expectation sharpens representations in the primary visual cortex. *Neuron*, *75*(2),
265–270. https://doi.org/10.1016/j.neuron.2012.04.034.

Kouider, S., de Gardelle, V., Sackur, J., & Dupoux, E. (2010). How rich is consciousness? The partial awareness hypothesis. *Trends in Cognitive Sciences*, *14*
(7), 301–307. https://doi.org/10.1016/j.tics.2010.04.006.

Kouider, S., Long, B., Le Stanc, L., et al. (2015). Neural dynamics of prediction and surprise in infants. *Nature Communications*, *6*, 8537. https://doi.org/ 10.1038/ncomms9537.

Kuhn, R. L. (2024). A landscape of consciousness: Toward a taxonomy of explanations and implications. *Progress in Biophysics and Molecular Biology*, *190*, 28–169. https://doi.org/10.1016/j.pbiomolbio.2023.12.003.

Kveraga, K., Boshyan, J., & Bar, M. (2007). Magnocellular projections as the trigger of top-down facilitation in recognition. *The Journal of Neuroscience*, *27*(48), 13232–13240. https://doi.org/10.1523/JNEUROSCI.3481-07.2007.

Lamme, V. A. (2003). Why visual attention and awareness are different. *Trends in Cognitive Sciences*, *7*(1), 12–18. https://doi.org/10.1016/s1364-6613(02) 00013-x.

Lamme, V. A. (2004). Separate neural definitions of visual consciousness and visual attention; a case for phenomenal awareness. *Neural Networks*, *17* (5–6), 861–872. https://doi.org/10.1016/j.neunet.2004.02.005.

Lamme, V. A. (2010). How neuroscience will change our view on consciousness. *Cognitive Neuroscience*, *1*(3), 204–220. https://doi.org/10.1080/17588921 003731586.

Lamme, V. A. (2018). Challenges for theories of consciousness: Seeing or knowing, the missing ingredient and how to deal with panpsychism. *Philosophical Transactions of the Royal Society B: Biological Sciences*, *373*(1755), 20170344.

Landman, R., Spekreijse, H., & Lamme, V. A. (2003). Large capacity storage of integrated objects before change blindness. *Vision Research*, *43*(2), 149–164. https://doi.org/10.1016/s0042-6989(02)00402-9.

Laureys, S. (2005). The neural correlate of (un)awareness: Lessons from the vegetative state. *Trends in Cognitive Sciences*, *9*(12), 556–559. https://doi .org/10.1016/j.tics.2005.10.010.

Laureys, S., Gosseries, O., & Tononi, G. (Eds.). (2015). *The neurology of consciousness: Cognitive neuroscience and neuropathology* (2nd ed.). London: Academic Press.

Lavie, N. (2005). Distracted and confused?: Selective attention under load. *Trends in Cognitive Sciences*, *9*(2), 75–82. https://doi.org/10.1016/j.tics .2004.12.004.

LeCun, Y., Bengio, Y., & Hinton, G. (2015). Deep learning. *Nature*, *521*, 436–444. https://doi.org/10.1038/nature14539.

Lenharo, M. (2023). Decades-long bet on consciousness ends – and it's philosopher 1, neuroscientist 0. *Nature*. *619*(7968), 14–15. https://doi.org/ 10.1038/d41586-023-02120-8.

Levin, D. T., Momen, N., Drivdahl, S. B., & Simons, D. J. (2000). Change blindness blindness: The metacognitive error of overestimating change-detection ability. *Visual Cognition*, *7*(1–3), 397–412. https://doi.org/10.1080/135062800394865.

Li, F. F., VanRullen, R., Koch, C., & Perona, P. (2002). Rapid natural scene categorization in the near absence of attention. *Proceedings of the National Academy of Sciences of the United States of America*, *99*(14), 9596–9601. https://doi.org/10.1073/pnas.092277599.

Logothetis, N. K., Leopold, D. A., & Sheinberg, D. L. (1996). What is rivalling during binocular rivalry? *Nature*, *380*(6575), 621–624. https://doi.org/10.1038/380621a0.

Luck, S. J., Chelazzi, L., Hillyard, S. A., & Desimone, R. (1997). Neural mechanisms of spatial selective attention in areas V1, V2, and V4 of macaque visual cortex. *Journal of Neurophysiology*, *77*(1), 24–42. https://doi.org/10.1152/jn.1997.77.1.24.

Luck, S., & Vogel, E. (1997). The capacity of visual working memory for features and conjunctions. *Nature*, *390*, 279–281. https://doi.org/10.1038/36846.

Mack, A., & Rock, I. (1998). *Inattentional blindness*. Cambridge, MA: MIT Press.

Mack, A., & Clarke, J. (2012). Gist perception requires attention. *Visual Cognition*, *20*(3), 300–327. https://doi.org/10.1080/13506285.2012.666578.

Mack, A., Erol, M., & Clarke, J. (2015). Iconic memory is not a case of attention-free awareness. *Consciousness and Cognition*, *33*, 291–299. https://doi.org/10.1016/j.concog.2014.12.016.

Mack, A., Erol, M., Clarke, J. , & Bert, J. (2016). No iconic memory without attention. *Consciousness and Cognition*, *40*, 1–8. https://doi.org/10.1016/j.concog.2015.12.006.

Mack, A., Clarke, J., Erol, M., & Bert, J. (2017). Scene incongruity and attention. *Consciousness and Cognition*, *48*, 87–103. https://doi.org/10.1016/j.concog.2016.10.010.

Marr, D. (1982). *Vision: A computational investigation into the human representation and processing of visual information*. Cambridge, MA: W. H. Freeman.

Martens, S., & Wyble, B. (2010). The attentional blink: Past, present, and future of a blind spot in perceptual awareness. *Neuroscience and Biobehavioral Reviews*, *34*(6), 947–957. https://doi.org/10.1016/j.neubiorev.2009.12.005.

Martínez, A., Teder-Salejarvi, W., & Hillyard, S. A. (2007). Spatial attention facilitates selection of illusory objects: Evidence from event-related brain potentials. *Brain Research*, *1139*, 143. https://doi.org/10.1016/j.brainres.2006.12.056.

Mashour, G. A., Roelfsema, P., Changeux, J. P., & Dehaene, S. (2020). Conscious processing and the global neuronal workspace hypothesis. *Neuron*, *105*(5), 776–798.

McMains, S. A., & Kastner, S. (2010). Defining the units of competition: Influences of perceptual organization on competitive interactions in human visual cortex. *Journal of Cognitive Neuroscience*, *22*(11), 2417–2426. https://doi.org/10.1162/jocn.2009.21391.

McNair, N. A., Goodbourn, P. T., Shone, L. T., & Harris, I. M. (2017). Summary statistics in the attentional blink. *Attention, Perception, & Psychophysics*, *79*, 100–116.

Mehrpour, V., Martinez-Trujillo, J. C., & Treue, S. (2020). Attention amplifies neural representations of changes in sensory input at the expense of perceptual accuracy. *Nature Communications*, *11*(1), 2128.

Melloni, L., Mudrik, L., Pitts, M., et al. (2023). An adversarial collaboration protocol for testing contrasting predictions of global neuronal workspace and integrated information theory. *PloS One*, *18*(2), e0268577. https://doi.org/10.1371/journal.pone.0268577.

Memmert, D. (2006). The effects of eye movements, age, and expertise on inattentional blindness. *Consciousness and Cognition*, *15*(3), 620–627. https://doi.org/10.1016/j.concog.2006.01.001.

Millidge, B., Seth, A., & Buckley, C. L. (2022). Predictive coding: A theoretical and experimental review. arXiv preprint arXiv:2107.12979.

Most, S. B., Chun, M. M., Widders, D. M., & Zald, D. H. (2005). Attentional rubbernecking: Cognitive control and personality in emotion-induced blindness. *Psychonomic Bulletin & Review*, *12*(4), 654–661. https://doi.org/10.3758/bf03196754.

Most, S. B., Scholl, B. J., Clifford, E. R., & Simons, D. J. (2005). What you see is what you set: Sustained inattentional blindness and the capture of awareness. *Psychological Review*, *112*(1), 217–242. https://doi.org/10.1037/0033-295X.112.1.217.

Most, S. B., Simons, D. J., Scholl, B. J., Jimenez, R., Clifford, E., & Chabris, C. F. (2001). How not to be seen: The contribution of similarity and selective ignoring to sustained inattentional blindness. *Psychological Science*, *12*(1), 9–17.

Mudrik, L., Breska, A., Lamy, D., & Deouell, L. Y. (2011). Integration without awareness: Expanding the limits of unconscious processing. *Psychological Science*, *22*(6), 764–770. https://doi.org/10.1177/0956797611408736.

Mudrik, L., & Koch, C. (2013). Differential processing of invisible congruent and incongruent scenes: A case for unconscious integration. *Journal of Vision*, *13*(13), 24. https://doi.org/10.1167/13.13.24.

Mumford, D. (1992). On the computational architecture of the neocortex. II. The role of cortico-cortical loops. *Biological Cybernetics*, *66*(3), 241–251. https://doi.org/10.1007/BF00198477.

Munneke, J., Brentari, V., & Peelen, M. V. (2013). The influence of scene context on object recognition is independent of attentional focus. *Frontiers in Psychology*, *4*, 552. https://doi.org/10.3389/fpsyg.2013.00552.

Naccache, L. (2018). Why and how access consciousness can account for phenomenal consciousness. *Philosophical Transactions of the Royal Society of London: Series B, Biological sciences*, *373*(1755), 20170357. https://doi.org/10.1098/rstb.2017.0357.

Nagel, T. (1974). What is it like to be a bat? *The Philosophical Review*, *83*(4), 435–450. https://doi.org/10.2307/2183914.

Neisser, U. (1967). *Cognitive psychology*. New York: Appleton-Century-Crofts.

Neisser, U., & Becklen, R. (1975). Selective looking: Attending to visually specified events. *Cognitive Psychology*, *7*(4), 480–494. https://doi.org/10.1016/0010-0285(75)90019-5.

Noah, S., & Mangun, G. R. (2020). Recent evidence that attention is necessary, but not sufficient, for conscious perception. *Annals of the New York Academy of Sciences*, *1464*(1), 52–63. https://doi.org/10.1111/nyas.14030.

Noë, A. (Ed.). (2002). *Is the visual world a grand illusion?* Exeter, UK: Imprint Academic.

Oliva, A. (2005). Gist of the scene. *Neurobiology of Attention*, 251–256. https://doi.org/10.1016/B978-012375731-9/50045-8.

Oliva, A., & Torralba, A. (2006). Building the gist of a scene: The role of global image features in recognition. *Progress in Brain Research*, *155*, 23–36. https://doi.org/10.1016/S0079-6123(06)55002-2.

Oliva, A., & Torralba, A. (2007). The role of context in object recognition. *Trends in Cognitive Sciences*, *11*(12), 520–527. https://doi.org/10.1016/j.tics.2007.09.009.

Olivers, C. N., & Meeter, M. (2008). A boost and bounce theory of temporal attention. *Psychological Review*, *115*(4), 836–863. https://doi.org/10.1037/a0013395.

Olkkonen, M., Hansen, T., & Gegenfurtner, K. R. (2008). Color appearance of familiar objects: Effects of object shape, texture, and illumination changes. *Journal of Vision*, *8*(5), 1–16. https://doi.org/10.1167/8.5.13.

O'Regan, J. K. (1992). Solving the 'real' mysteries of visual perception: The world as an outside memory. *Canadian Journal of Psychology*, *46*(3), 461–488. https://doi.org/10.1037/h0084327.

Otten, M., Seth, A. K., & Pinto, Y. (2023). Seeing Ɔ, remembering C: Illusions in short-term memory. *PloS One*, *18*(4), e0283257. https://doi.org/10.1371/journal.pone.0283257.

Overgaard, M. (2018). Phenomenal consciousness and cognitive access. *Philosophical Transactions of the Royal Society B: Biological Sciences*, *373*(1755), 20170353.

Overgaard, M., & Overgaard, R. (2010). Neural correlates of contents and levels of consciousness. *Frontiers in Psychology*, *1*, 164.

Palmer, S. E. (1975). The effects of contextual scenes on the identification of objects. *Memory & Cognition*, *3*(5), 519–526. https://doi.org/10.3758/BF03197524.

Panichello, M. F., Cheung, O. S., & Bar, M. (2013). Predictive feedback and conscious visual experience. *Frontiers in Psychology*, *3*, 620. https://doi.org/10.3389/fpsyg.2012.00620.

Peelen, M. V., Berlot, E., & de Lange, F. P. (2024). Predictive processing of scenes and objects. *Nature Reviews Psychology*, *3*, 13–26. https://doi.org/10.1038/s44159-023-00254-0.

Persuh, M., Genzer, B., & Melara, R. D. (2012). Iconic memory requires attention. *Frontiers in Human Neuroscience*, *6*, Article 126. https://doi.org/10.3389/fnhum.2012.00126.

Persuh, M., & Melara, R. D. (2016). Barack Obama Blindness (BOB): Absence of visual awareness to a single object. *Frontiers in Human Neuroscience*, *10*, 118. https://doi.org/10.3389/fnhum.2016.00118.

Pinto, Y., van Gaal, S., de Lange, F. P., Lamme, V. A., & Seth, A. K. (2015). Expectations accelerate entry of visual stimuli into awareness. *Journal of Vision*, *15*(8), 13. https://doi.org/10.1167/15.8.13.

Pitts, M. A., Martínez, A., & Hillyard, S. A. (2012). Visual processing of contour patterns under conditions of inattentional blindness. *Journal of Cognitive Neuroscience*, *24*(2), 287–303. https://doi.org/10.1162/jocn_a_00111.

Pitts, M. A., Lutsyshyna, L. A., & Hillyard, S. A. (2018). The relationship between attention and consciousness: An expanded taxonomy and implications for 'no-report' paradigms. *Philosophical Transactions of the Royal Society of London: Series B, Biological sciences*, *373*(1755), 20170348. https://doi.org/10.1098/rstb.2017.0348.

Posner, M. I. (1980). Orienting of attention. *The Quarterly Journal of Experimental Psychology*, *32*(1), 3–25. https://doi.org/10.1080/00335558008248231.

Potter, M. C., Wyble, B., Hagmann, C. E., & McCourt, E. S. (2014). Detecting meaning in RSVP at 13 ms per picture. *Attention, Perception & Psychophysics*, *76*(2), 270–279. https://doi.org/10.3758/s13414-013-0605-z.

Powers III, A. R., Kelley, M., & Corlett, P. R. (2016). Hallucinations as top-down effects on perception. *Biological psychiatry: Cognitive Neuroscience and Neuroimaging, 1*(5), 393–400. https://doi.org/10.1016/j.bpsc.2016.04.003.

Powers, A. R., Mathys, C., & Corlett, P. R. (2017). Pavlovian conditioning-induced hallucinations result from overweighting of perceptual priors. *Science, 357*(6351), 596–600. https://doi.org/10.1126/science.aan3458.

Press, C., Kok, P., & Yon, D. (2020). The perceptual prediction paradox. *Trends in Cognitive Sciences, 24*(1), 13–24. https://doi.org/10.1016/j.tics.2019.11.003.

Raffone, A., Srinivasan, N., & van Leeuwen, C. (2014). The interplay of attention and consciousness in visual search, attentional blink and working memory consolidation. *Philosophical Transactions of the Royal Society of London: Series B, Biological Sciences, 369*(1641), 20130215. https://doi.org/10.1098/rstb.2013.0215.

Railo, H., Koivisto, M., & Revonsuo, A. (2011). Tracking the processes behind conscious perception: A review of event-related potential correlates of visual consciousness. *Consciousness and Cognition, 20*(3), 972–983. https://doi.org/10.1016/j.concog.2011.03.019.

Rao, R. P., & Ballard, D. H. (1999). Predictive coding in the visual cortex: A functional interpretation of some extra-classical receptive-field effects. *Nature Neuroscience, 2*(1), 79–87.

Raymond, J. E., Shapiro, K. L., & Arnell, K. M. (1992). Temporary suppression of visual processing in an RSVP task: An attentional blink? *Journal of Experimental Psychology: Human Perception and Performance, 18*(3), 849–860. https://doi.org/10.1037//0096-1523.18.3.849.

Rees, G., Kreiman, G., & Koch, C. (2002). Neural correlates of consciousness in humans. *Nature reviews: Neuroscience, 3*(4), 261–270. https://doi.org/10.1038/nrn783.

Rees, G., Russell, C., Frith, C. D., & Driver, J. (1999). Inattentional blindness versus inattentional amnesia for fixated but ignored words. *Science, 286* (5449), 2504-2507.

Rensink, R. A., O'Regan, J. K., & Clark, J. J. (1997). To see or not to see: The need for attention to perceive changes in scenes. *Psychological Science, 8*(5), 368–373. https://doi.org/10.1111/j.1467-9280.1997.tb00427.x.

Rensink, R. A. (2000). The dynamic representation of scenes. *Visual Cognition, 7*(1–3), 17–42. https://doi.org/10.1080/135062800394667.

Rensink, R. A. (2004). Visual sensing without seeing. *Psychological Science, 15*(1), 27–32. https://doi.org/10.1111/j.0963-7214.2004.01501005.x.

Reynolds, J. H., & Chelazzi, L. (2004). Attentional modulation of visual processing. *Annual Review of Neuroscience, 27*, 611–647. https://doi.org/10.1146/annurev.neuro.26.041002.131039.

Reynolds, J. H., & Heeger, D. J. (2009). The normalization model of attention. *Neuron, 61*(2), 168–185. https://doi.org/10.1016/j.neuron.2009.01.002.

Rousselet, G., Joubert, O., & Fabre-Thorpe, M. (2005). How long to get to the 'gist' of real-world natural scenes? *Visual Cognition, 12*(6), 852–877.

Rousselet, G. A., Macé, M. J., & Fabre-Thorpe, M. (2003). Is it an animal? Is it a human face? Fast processing in upright and inverted natural scenes. *Journal of Vision, 3*(6), 440–455. https://doi.org/10.1167/3.6.5.

Saenz, M., Buracas, G. T., & Boynton, G. M. (2002). Global effects of feature-based attention in human visual cortex. *Nature Neuroscience, 5*(7), 631–632. https://doi.org/10.1038/nn876.

Schelonka, K., Graulty, C., Canseco-Gonzalez, E., & Pitts, M. A. (2017). ERP signatures of conscious and unconscious word and letter perception in an inattentional blindness paradigm. *Consciousness and Cognition, 54*, 56–71.

Scholl, B. J., Simons, D. J., & Levin, D. T. (2004). 'Change blindness' blindness: An implicit measure of a metacognitive error. In D. T. Levin (Ed.), *Thinking and seeing: Visual metacognition in adults and children* (pp. 145–164). Cambridge, MA: MIT Press.

Sergent, C., & Dehaene, S. (2004). Is consciousness a gradual phenomenon? Evidence for an all-or-none bifurcation during the attentional blink. *Psychological Science, 15*(11), 720–728.

Sergent, C., Baillet, S., & Dehaene, S. (2005). Timing of the brain events underlying access to consciousness during the attentional blink. *Nature Neuroscience, 8*(10), 1391–1400. https://doi.org/10.1038/nn1549.

Sergent, C., Wyart, V., Babo-Rebelo, M., Cohen, L., Naccache, L., & Tallon-Baudry, C. (2013). Cueing attention after the stimulus is gone can retrospectively trigger conscious perception. *Current Biology, 23*(2), 150–155.

Seriès, P., & Seitz, A. R. (2013). Learning what to expect (in visual perception). *Frontiers in Human Neuroscience, 7*, Article 668. https://doi.org/10.3389/fnhum.2013.00668.

Seth, A. K. (2021). *Being you: A new science of consciousness*. London: Faber & Faber.

Seth, A. K., & Hohwy, J. (2021). Predictive processing as an empirical theory for consciousness science. *Cognitive Neuroscience, 12*(2), 89–90. https://doi.org/10.1080/17588928.2020.1838467.

Seth, A. K., & Bayne, T. (2022). Theories of consciousness. *Nature Reviews Neuroscience, 23*, 439–452. https://doi.org/10.1038/s41583-022-00587-4.

Shafto, J. P., & Pitts, M. A. (2015). Neural signatures of conscious face perception in an inattentional blindness paradigm. *The Journal of Neuroscience, 35*(31), 10940–10948. https://doi.org/10.1523/JNEUROSCI.0145-15.2015.

Simons, D. J., & Levin, D.T. (1998). Failure to detect changes to people during a real-world interaction. *Psychonomic Bulletin & Review, 5*, 644–649. https://doi.org/10.3758/BF03208840.

Simons, D. J., & Chabris, C. F. (1999). Gorillas in our midst: Sustained inattentional blindness for dynamic events. *Perception, 28*(9), 1059–1074. https://doi.org/10.1068/p281059.

Simons, D. J., & Jensen, M. S. (2009). The effects of individual differences and task difficulty on inattentional blindness. *Psychonomic Bulletin & Review, 16*(2), 398–403. https://doi.org/10.3758/PBR.16.2.398.

Simons, D. J., & Levin, D. T. (1997). Change blindness. *Trends in Cognitive Sciences, 1*(7), 261–267.

Simons, D. J., & Rensink, R. A. (2005). Change blindness: Past, present, and future. *Trends in Cognitive Sciences, 9*(1), 16–20.

Sligte, I. G., Vandenbroucke, A. R., Scholte, H. S., & Lamme, V. A. (2010). Detailed sensory memory, sloppy working memory. *Frontiers in Psychology, 1*, 175. https://doi.org/10.3389/fpsyg.2010.00175.

Sperling, G. (1960). The information available in brief visual presentations. *Psychological Monographs: General and Applied, 74*(11), 1–29. https://doi.org/10.1037/h0093759.

Sterzer, P., Haynes, J. D., & Rees, G. (2008). Fine-scale activity patterns in high-level visual areas encode the category of invisible objects. *Journal of Vision, 8*(15), 1–12. https://doi.org/10.1167/8.15.10.

Sterzer, P., Kleinschmidt, A., & Rees, G. (2009). The neural bases of multistable perception. *Trends in Cognitive Sciences, 13*(7), 310–318. https://doi.org/10.1016/j.tics.2009.04.006.

Summerfield, C., & de Lange, F. P. (2014). Expectation in perceptual decision making: Neural and computational mechanisms. *Nature Reviews Neuroscience, 15*(11), 745–756. https://doi.org/10.1038/nrn3838

Summerfield, C., & Egner, T. (2009). Expectation (and attention) in visual cognition. *Trends in Cognitive Sciences, 13*(9), 403–409. https://doi.org/10.1016/j.tics.2009.06.003.

Suzuki, K., Roseboom, W., Schwartzman, D. J., & Seth, A. K. (2017). A deep-dream virtual reality platform for studying altered perceptual phenomenology. *Scientific Reports, 7*(1), 15982. https://doi.org/10.1038/s41598-017-16316-2.

Swanson, L. R. (2016). The predictive processing paradigm has roots in Kant. *Frontiers in Systems Neuroscience, 10*, 79. https://doi.org/10.3389/fnsys.2016.00079.

Tachmatzidou, O., & Vatakis, A. (2023). Attention and schema violations of real world scenes differentially modulate time perception. *Scientific Reports, 13*(1), 10002.

Tong, F., Meng, M., & Blake, R. (2006). Neural bases of binocular rivalry. *Trends in Cognitive Sciences*, *10*(11), 502–511. https://doi.org/10.1016/j.tics.2006.09.003.

Tononi, G., & Koch, C. (2008). The neural correlates of consciousness: An update. *Annals of the New York Academy of Sciences*, *1124*(1), 239–261.

Treisman, A. M., & Gelade, G. (1980). A feature-integration theory of attention. *Cognitive Psychology*, *12*(1), 97–136. https://doi.org/10.1016/0010-0285(80)90005-5.

Tsuchiya, N., & Koch, C. (2014). On the relationship between consciousness and attention. In M. S. Gazzaniga, & G. R. Mangun (Eds.), *The cognitive neurosciences* (5th ed., pp. 839–853). Cambridge, MA: MIT Press. https://doi.org/10.7551/mitpress/9504.003.0092.

Tsuchiya, N., Wilke, M., Frässle, S., & Lamme, V. A. F. (2015). No-report paradigms: Extracting the true neural correlates of consciousness. *Trends in Cognitive Sciences*, *19*(12), 757–770. https://doi.org/10.1016/j.tics.2015.10.002.

Valsecchi, M., & Gegenfurtner, K. R. (2016). Dynamic re-calibration of perceived size in fovea and periphery through predictable size changes. *Current Biology: CB*, *26*(1), 59–63. https://doi.org/10.1016/j.cub.2015.10.067.

Vandenbroucke, A. R. E., Sligte, I. G., Barrett, A. B., et al. (2014). Accurate metacognition for visual sensory memory representations. *Psychological Science*, *25*(4), 861–873. https://doi.org/10.1177/0956797613516146.

Vandenbroucke, A. R., Sligte, I. G., Fahrenfort, J. J., Ambroziak, K. B., & Lamme, V. A. (2012). Non-attended representations are perceptual rather than unconscious in nature. *PLoS One*, *7*(11), e50042.

Velmans, M. (2010). *Understanding consciousness*. London: Routledge.

Ward, E. J., & Scholl, B. J. (2015). Inattentional blindness reflects limitations on perception, not memory: Evidence from repeated failures of awareness. *Psychonomic Bulletin & Review*, *22*(3), 722–727. https://doi.org/10.3758/s13423-014-0745-8.

Ward, E. J. (2018). Downgraded phenomenology: How conscious overflow lost its richness. *Philosophical Transactions of the Royal Society of London: Series B, Biological sciences*, *373*(1755), 20170355. https://doi.org/10.1098/rstb.2017.0355.

Webster, K., Clarke, J., Mack, A., & Ro, T. (2018). Effects of canonical color, luminance, and orientation on sustained inattentional blindness for scenes. *Attention, Perception, & Psychophysics*, *80*(7), 1833–1846. https://doi.org/10.3758/s13414-018-1558-z.

Witzel, C., & Gegenfurtner, K. R. (2013). Categorical sensitivity to color differences. *Journal of Vision*, *13*(7), Article 1. https://doi.org/10.1167/13.7.1.

Wolfe, J. M. (1999). Inattentional amnesia. In V. Coltheart (Ed.), *Fleeting memories* (pp. 71–94). Cambridge, MA: MIT Press.

Wood, K., & Simons, D. J. (2017). The role of similarity in inattentional blindness: Selective enhancement, selective suppression, or both?†. *Visual Cognition*, *25*(9–10), 972–980. https://doi.org/10.1080/13506285.2017.1365791.

Yeshurun, Y., & Carrasco, M. (1998). Attention improves or impairs visual performance by enhancing spatial resolution. *Nature*, *396*(6706), 72–75. https://doi.org/10.1038/23936.

Yeshurun, Y., & Levy, L. (2003). Transient spatial attention degrades temporal resolution. *Psychological Science*, *14*(3), 225–231. https://doi.org/10.1111/1467-9280.02436.

Yon, D., & Frith, C. D. (2021). Precision and the Bayesian brain. *Current Biology*, *31*(17), R1026–R1032. https://doi.org/10.1016/j.cub.2021.07.044.

Yon, D., & Press, C. (2017). Predicted action consequences are perceptually facilitated before cancellation. *Journal of Experimental Psychology: Human Perception and Performance*, *43*(6), 1073–1083. https://doi.org/10.1037/xhp0000385.

Zivony, A., & Lamy, D. (2022). What processes are disrupted during the attentional blink? An integrative review of event-related potential research. *Psychonomic Bulletin & Review*, *29*(2), 394–414.

For Johnny

Cambridge Elements ☰

Perception

James T. Enns
The University of British Columbia

Editor James T. Enns is Professor at the University of British Columbia, where he researches the interaction of perception, attention, emotion, and social factors. He has previously been Editor of the *Journal of Experimental Psychology: Human Perception and Performance* and an associate editor at *Psychological Science, Consciousness and Cognition, Attention Perception & Psychophysics,* and *Visual Cognition.*

About the Series
The modern study of human perception includes event perception, bidirectional influences between perception and action, music, language, the integration of the senses, human action observation, and the important roles of emotion, motivation, and social factors. Each Element in the series combines authoritative literature reviews of foundational topics with forward-looking presentations of the recent developments on a given topic.

Cambridge Elements ☰

Perception